DEDICATION

I want to extend a heartfelt thanks to my dear husband Reg, who ate his way through another book's worth of salads. He endured the attempts that never made it into this collection with much grace and joked that he's grown cauliflower ears and a carrot nose. I also owe a nod to the many friends and family who have joined me at the dinner table, because that is really what it's all about in the end.

The *Ultimate* SALAD Book

CHANTAL LASCARIS

Published in 2021 by Struik Lifestyle, an imprint of Penguin Random House
South Africa (Pty) Ltd
Company Reg. No. 1953/000441/07
The Estuaries, 4 Oxbow Crescent, Century Avenue, Century City 7441,
Cape Town, South Africa
PO Box 1144, Cape Town, 8000, South Africa
www.penguinrandomhouse.co.za

Reprinted in 2022

PUBLISHER: Beverley Dodd
MANAGING EDITOR and INDEXER: Cecilia Barfield
EDITOR: Bronwen Maynier
DESIGNER: Helen Henn
PROOFREADER: Jennifer Leak
PHOTOGRAPHER: Donna Lewis
PHOTOGRAPHER'S ASSISTANT: Malizo Masumpa
STYLIST: Caro Alberts
ASSISTANTS: Ellah Maepa

Reproduction: Studio Repro, Cape Town
Printed and bound in China by C&C Offset Printing Co., Ltd

ISBN 978-1-48590-081-8

CONTENTS

Introduction   6

Classic Salads   8

3-Ingredient Salads   16

Vegetarian Salads   28

Fish & Seafood Salads   62

Poultry Salads   96

Meat Salads   124

Fruity Salads   154

Dressings   172

Index   174

SERVINGS: Please note that all recipes serve 4 people.

INTRODUCTION

It's time for the salad to take centre stage! Too often relegated to the sidelines of the meal, the humble but healthy salad can be so much more. I feel the traditional view of what a salad can be is far too narrow, but I hope to push those boundaries and bring salads over and onto the main dish. The creativity and variety of salads that you can craft in your kitchen is truly astonishing.

There's so much more to salad than a handful of lettuce leaves and a few tomatoes. What it all boils down to is simple, nourishing and delicious meals with plenty of nutrient-dense ingredients. All those good and healthy things, like leafy green vegetables, whole grains, seafood, poultry, beans, nuts and fruit. With this assortment of superb salads, you'll be eating them for breakfast, lunch, dinner and even dessert.

This book aims to be the definitive collection of salads, bringing international flavours to the South African kitchen. You'll find something in here for any occasion. While there are still plenty of quick and easy recipes to whip up at short notice as a side dish, many of these salads are bold enough to stand up on their own at the meal table or provide showstopper centrepieces to dazzle guests at a dinner party.

These salads range from traditional classics like the quintessential Greek salad through to far more elaborate dishes featuring exotic and unusual ingredients like duck, scallops and even crayfish. You'll find vibrant and flavourful side salads that shine as accompaniments or starters, protein-packed lunches that keep the body and mind nourished throughout the day, and deliciously dazzling main courses. There's a vast array of herbaceous and wholesome options to explore. With chapters dedicated to vegetarian, seafood, chicken, meat, classics, three-ingredient salads and even fruity sweet delights, there's something to suit any taste or mood.

This is also very much my own personal take and reflects my own journey. Since writing my first book, I've had the chance to really settle into life on my farm in Franschhoek, grow closer to nature and come to love my veggie and herb garden. This has deepened my appreciation for fresh ingredients and brought me more in tune with both the seasons and the seasonality of ingredients. It brings me such joy to add fresh-plucked herbs from the garden and it is something that you can do at home even with just a windowsill.

This is my first title outside of the *All Sorts of* series, but much like my previous books, *All Sorts of Salads*, *All Sorts of Healthy Dishes*, *All Sorts of One-Dish Wonders* and *All Sorts of Tapas*, there's a strong focus on eating healthily, giving you choice and using local ingredients where possible. This book is bigger and more ambitious, but I've also felt myself coming full circle. In putting together this collection, I've returned to my 'salad roots' with a broader view and incorporating elements from my other books. After all, salads are healthy meals, served in one dish, and can be eaten at any time of day.

Accompanied by stunning photographs that capture the bold flashes of colour and taste that jump off the plate, each page is a feast for the eyes, as well as the tummy. There's a recipe for every season and every occasion. Some are savoury and some are sweet. There are salads that are light and elegant, perfect for summer lunches with a glass or two of chilled white wine, or that are rich and hearty enough to pair with a red wine on a chilly evening.

As seasons change, so does availability, but don't ever let that hold you back. Please feel free to get creative and work with what you have and what you like best. Unlike baking, you won't risk a flop if you're a teaspoon short of an ingredient or add an extra handful of this or that.

I hope you enjoy this book as much as I enjoyed putting it together. I wish you many healthy and fun meals ahead. May your kitchen resound with the joy and laughter of those magical moments that come together when we gather for a meal with friends and loved ones.

Bon appetit!

Chantal Lascaris

Sometimes we don't feel all that adventurous or inspired and rather crave the comfort of a familiar dish. This tried-and-tested collection brings a taste of the traditional to the table. While these well-established salad recipes might have been made time and again around the world, they are certainly never boring.

They embody everything that we love most about salads: healthy, fresh, tasty and bursting with life. From a true Greek salad (without the lettuce) to a Waldorf salad, when it comes to the world's most famous salads, you will find a recipe to suit your taste right here.

These classic salads are the quintessential collection to have in your bag of cooking tricks. Eating colourful, nutritious food has never been easier or more delicious than with these cherished recipes.

Classic
Salads

Caprese Salad

This is one of my personal favourites. It's got the colours of the Italian flag, which I'm not sure was intentional considering it comes from the island of Capri in southern Italy. It's as chic as the women who grace the yachts moored along the Amalfi Coast. For a more traditional approach, present it in stacks with alternating slices of mozzarella and large ripe tomato.

350g small mixed tomatoes
200g bocconcini
a handful of fresh basil leaves

2 Tbsp basil pesto
¼ cup olive oil
salt and pepper to taste

1. Halve the tomatoes and gently tear the bocconcini.

2. Arrange the tomatoes and bocconcini on a plate.

3. Scatter over the basil leaves and place dollops of the basil pesto on top.

4. Generously drizzle with the olive oil and season well with salt and pepper.

Waldorf Salad

Although this salad was only invented in the 1950s at the Waldorf Astoria in New York, it quickly became a classic due to its delicious flavours and textures. It's the combination of the crunchy walnuts and sweet grapes, contrasting with the tangy dressing that makes it a winner. The lemon juice is a good way to keep the apples from discolouring. Apples discolour when exposed to air due to a chemical reaction and the low acidity in the lemon juice counteracts this process.

2 red apples
1 Tbsp lemon juice
1 cos lettuce
⅓ cup red grapes
3 stalks celery, sliced
½ cup roughly chopped walnuts

DRESSING
½ cup mayonnaise
2 Tbsp lemon juice
salt and pepper to taste

1. Thinly slice the apples and toss in the lemon juice.

2. Place the lettuce leaves on a platter or individual plates. Add the apple slices, grapes and celery, and scatter the walnuts on top.

3. Whisk the dressing ingredients and pour over the salad.

Bean Salad

I like to use extra-fine green beans in salads. They're sweeter and more tender. It's best to plunge them in ice water after cooking so that they retain their crisp, green colour and remain crunchy. There's nothing worse than limp green beans. This salad is perfect to make some time before serving, as the flavours mellow and deepen the longer you leave them. The mixture of colours is also a feast for the eyes.

200g butter beans
200g red kidney beans
100g fresh extra-fine green beans
½ red onion, finely chopped
½ red pepper, finely chopped
2 stalks celery, finely chopped

DRESSING
½ Tbsp honey
¼ cup olive oil
3 Tbsp white wine vinegar
½ tsp mustard powder
½ tsp dried basil
salt and pepper to taste

1. Drain and rinse the butter and kidney beans. Place the green beans in a saucepan of boiling water for about 2 minutes and then plunge into ice water to stop the cooking process. Top and tail the green beans and then cut them in half or thirds, depending on their size.

2. Toss all the beans with the red onion, red pepper and celery in a bowl.

3. Whisk the dressing ingredients and pour over the salad. Mix to coat well.

Greek Salad

You won't find a Greek taverna serving a Greek salad with lettuce and you won't find one here either. More often than not they're also served with a large chunk of salty feta, not crumbled over. This way you appreciate the true flavour of the cheese, which balances the sweetness of the ripe tomatoes. The other Greek staple is olives, but don't be tempted to pick one straight off the tree - they're incredibly bitter and need to be soaked in brine for quite some time.

4 large ripe tomatoes, sliced into wedges
½ large cucumber, sliced
½ red onion, sliced into rings
15 kalamata olives
150g feta

DRESSING
¼ cup olive oil
2 Tbsp lemon juice
1 Tbsp chopped fresh origanum or 1 tsp dried
1 clove garlic, crushed
salt and pepper to taste

1. Combine the tomatoes, cucumber, red onion and olives in a bowl.

2. Place the blocks of feta on top.

3. Whisk the dressing ingredients and check the seasoning.

4. Pour the dressing over the salad and chill in the fridge until ready to serve.

Creamy Coleslaw

Sometimes cabbage gets a bad rap because it contains raffinose, a complex sugar that causes excess gas. But this much maligned vegetable is actually full of goodness. It's got high levels of vitamin K, which is good for the brain, and it even has anti-carcinogenic properties that counteract the effects of carcinogens, which cause degeneration and cancers in living tissue. So don't toss out the cabbage just yet.

1 cup shredded white cabbage
1 cup grated carrot
½ cup grated or julienned apple
2 spring onions, finely chopped
¼ cup raisins
3 Tbsp chopped peanuts

DRESSING
2 Tbsp olive oil
¼ cup light mayonnaise
1 Tbsp lemon juice
2 Tbsp orange juice
salt and pepper to taste

1. Mix the cabbage, carrot and apple in a bowl.

2. Add the spring onions, raisins and peanuts, and mix to combine.

3. Whisk the dressing ingredients and check the seasoning.

4. Pour the dressing over the salad, tossing well to ensure everything is well coated.

Onion Salad

This salad is certainly a classic in my household, as it was in my mom's and my grandmother's. I've been eating it for as long as I can remember. The best part is that it lasts a couple of days in the fridge, so it's perfect for camping and picnics. It might not be the healthiest of salads with the sugar, but it's certainly worth it.

500g small onions, sliced
2 cups boiling water
chopped chives for garnishing

DRESSING
½ cup white sugar
½ tsp salt
2 tsp mustard powder
½ cup white wine vinegar
1 Tbsp cornflour
2 eggs

1. Place the onions in a microwavable bowl and cover with the boiling water. Microwave on high for 6–8 minutes until the onions are soft. Drain and set aside.

2. For the dressing, combine all the ingredients in another microwavable bowl and whisk well. Microwave on high for 2–3 minutes until thick, stirring often.

3. Pour the dressing over the onions, ensuring they are well coated, and then garnish with chopped fresh chives.

When cooking, I often find myself adding a bit of this and a bit of that and then being tempted to add just a little bit more. Sometimes, though, less is more and salads are no exception. You might worry that a salad with only three ingredients won't be tasty enough, but the recipes here are anything but bland.

I really enjoy the simplicity of these salads and how quickly some of them come together. They're perfect for when unexpected guests drop in or when you arrive home late from work dog-tired but hungry for something healthy.

It's especially important when using so few ingredients to use the freshest in-season produce you can find, so that each ingredient's flavours and textures really stand out. Think beautifully plump, ruby-red tomatoes for the tomato, onion and ricotta salad or unblemished, creamy, soft avocados for the avocado, corn and spring onion salad.

No matter which of these salads you choose, you'll be sure to find they're quick, fresh, vibrant and perfect for a busy lifestyle.

3 Ingredient Salads

Beets Three Ways, Baby Marrow and Rocket

This is beetroot heaven: presented in three different ways, all within the same dish. Roasted, pickled and grilled, beetroot is such a versatile root vegetable. It's extremely healthy too, rich in vitamin C, fibre and nutrients, and low in calories. All the more reason to enjoy it, don't you think?

6 medium baby marrows, sliced into ribbons
2 tsp olive oil
9 medium beetroots
1 cup red wine vinegar
3 Tbsp brown sugar
salt and pepper to taste
2–3 cups rocket

DRESSING
1 tsp red wine vinegar
¼ cup water
salt and pepper to taste

1. Preheat the oven to 220°C.

2. Place the baby marrow ribbons on a greased baking sheet, drizzle over the olive oil and roast for a few minutes until they start to char. Remove and allow to cool.

3. Bring a saucepan of water to the boil and cook the unpeeled beetroots for about 30 minutes or until they've softened. Drain and set aside to cool, then peel.

4. Cut a third of the beetroots into cubes and place in a sealable bag along with the red wine vinegar, sugar, salt and pepper, and refrigerate for at least 30 minutes. For best results, leave overnight.

5. Finely slice another third of the beetroots, place on a greased baking sheet and grill until they start to char. Remove and allow to cool.

6. Using a hand blender, purée the balance of the beetroots with the dressing ingredients.

7. Place the rocket on a platter, drizzle over half the beetroot purée and toss to coat.

8. Scatter over the baby marrow ribbons, beetroot cubes and beetroot slices, pour over the balance of the purée and serve.

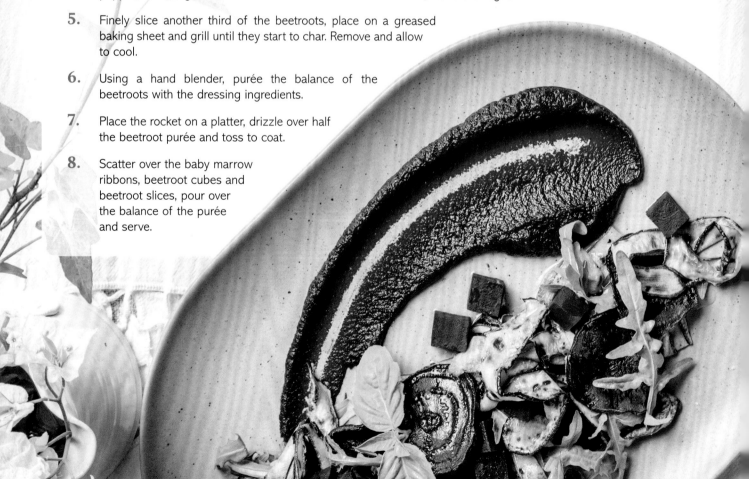

Corn, Spring Onion and Avocado

My favourite way of eating corn is by grilling it first, preferably over a hot fire. It produces a subtle smokiness that always reminds me of summer. But sometimes an open fire isn't available, so grilling the corn using an oven or gas top is the next best option. It still brings out the sweetness of the corn, which is juxtaposed with the strong spring onion and rounded off with the creamy avocado. Bliss.

2 corn on the cob
2–3 avocados
⅓ cup sliced spring onion

DRESSING
¼ cup olive oil
2 tsp lemon juice
1 tsp honey
salt and pepper to taste

1. Remove the husks from the corncobs and grill until charred.

2. Slice the corn off the cobs and place in a serving bowl.

3. Peel and chop the avocados and add to the corn.

4. Scatter over the spring onion.

5. Whisk the dressing ingredients, pour over the salad and toss gently to combine.

Peppers, Butternut and Mozzarella

Mozzarella di bufala is traditionally a southern Italian cheese made from the curd of buffalo milk. It's often known as 'the pearl of the table', for many reasons. It's round or oval in shape and is very white, wet and shiny, just like a pearl. Being a fresh, moist cheese, it's perfect for absorbing the flavours around it, like the smokiness from the roasted peppers and the herb dressing in this salad. For me, it's true Mediterranean royalty.

2 cups cubed butternut
olive oil for drizzling
1 large buffalo mozzarella ball
1 cup store-bought roasted red and yellow
   pepper slices

DRESSING
¼ cup olive oil
2 Tbsp roughly chopped fresh basil
2 Tbsp roughly chopped fresh mint
1 tsp white wine vinegar
salt and pepper to taste

1. Preheat the oven to 190°C.

2. Place the butternut cubes onto a greased baking sheet and drizzle with some olive oil.

3. Roast the butternut until the edges start to char and the butternut has softened. Remove and set aside to cool.

4. Break up the mozzarella and toss with the butternut and roasted pepper slices in a bowl.

5. Using a hand blender, whizz the dressing ingredients and drizzle over the salad.

Avocado, Artichoke and Tomato

Fresh artichokes, although absolutely delicious, are quite difficult to eat. That's why I enjoy using store-bought roasted artichokes, which have the added benefit of being already roasted and seasoned. They work especially well here, as the oil is used as part of the dressing and the earthy flavours blend seamlessly with the creamy avocado and sweet tomatoes. Cooking and marinating fresh artichokes softens the leaves and intensifies the overall flavour.

2–3 avocados, sliced
1 cup store-bought roasted artichoke pieces
1 cup small mixed tomatoes, halved
   depending on size

DRESSING
2 Tbsp oil from roasted artichokes
½ Tbsp sherry vinegar
½ tsp brown sugar
½ tsp dried origanum

1. Combine the salad ingredients in a bowl.

2. Whisk the dressing ingredients, pour over the salad and toss gently to combine.

Cauliflower, Onion and Coriander

This is a delicious way to present cauliflower. The aromatic spices are quintessential curry ingredients, and paired with the cauliflower, you have all the components of a curry, presented in salad form. The coriander adds the last flourishing curry touch to this dish. Coriander leaves, otherwise known as cilantro, are often used in Indian cuisine to provide a fresh, lemony flavour to a spicy curry.

1 large head cauliflower (about 500g florets)
1 tsp ground coriander
1 tsp ground cumin
2 tsp medium curry powder
2 tsp paprika
1 medium onion, roughly chopped

salt and pepper to taste
¼ cup olive oil, plus 2 Tbsp for serving
1 ½ Tbsp red wine vinegar
¼ cup roughly chopped fresh coriander,
    stalks removed

1. Preheat the oven to 220°C.

2. If using a full cauliflower head, cut into florets.

3. In a bowl, mix the ground coriander, cumin, curry powder and paprika.

4. Add the cauliflower florets and chopped onion to the spices and toss well. Season with salt and pepper.

5. Add the ¼ cup olive oil and the red wine vinegar and toss until the florets and onion are well coated.

6. Evenly spread the coated cauliflower and onion on a greased baking sheet. Bake for about 20 minutes, tossing halfway, until the cauliflower is tender and starts to caramelise. Remove, allow to cool and place in a serving bowl.

7. Scatter over the chopped fresh coriander and drizzle over the 2 Tbsp olive oil.

Mushroom, Parsley and Parmesan

Honey mustard is sweet, tangy and creamy all at the same time, and is a delicious addition to this simple salad. It works well with the meaty mushrooms and salty Parmesan. It's important to use the freshest mushrooms and the best-quality cheese you can find, because the flavours of these two ingredients really stand out. I like the addition of parsley, as it adds a dash of colour as well as providing extra health benefits, such as improving digestion, among others.

1 cup sliced brown mushrooms
1 cup sliced button mushrooms
1 cup shaved Parmesan
1 cup loosely packed fresh parsley, chopped

DRESSING
¼ cup olive oil
1 tsp white wine vinegar
½ tsp honey mustard
salt and pepper to taste

1. Mix the mushrooms and Parmesan in a bowl and scatter over the parsley.

2. Whisk the dressing ingredients, pour over the salad and toss to combine.

Tomato, Onion and Ricotta

Originally, ricotta was made from whey, whereas most other cheeses are made from curd. Nowadays, however, it's often made the same way as the rest. The main difference is that ricotta is a fresh cheese with a lot of moisture in it, which provides that delicious light flavour. This means it's also more perishable compared to a harder, dry cheese like Parmesan. I enjoy teaming creamy ricotta with sweet tomatoes and tangy red onions to provide a simple, yet tasty side salad.

2 cups halved small mixed tomatoes
⅔ cup thinly sliced red onion
⅔ cup roughly broken ricotta
chopped fresh origanum for garnishing

DRESSING
¼ cup olive oil
2 tsp honey
2 tsp red wine vinegar
½ tsp crushed garlic
½ tsp dried origanum
salt and pepper to taste

1. Preheat the oven to 180°C.

2. Place the tomatoes on a greased baking sheet and roast until they start to char. Remove and allow to cool.

3. Place the tomatoes, red onion and ricotta in a bowl.

4. Whisk the dressing ingredients and pour over the salad. Toss to combine.

5. Place in the fridge for about 30 minutes to allow the flavours to develop.

6. When ready to serve, garnish with chopped fresh origanum.

Cucumber, Onion and Walnut

Although, botanically speaking, cucumbers are fruit, we often associate them with vegetables. Pickling them is a wonderful way of giving new flavour to what is otherwise quite a common ingredient. The addition of walnuts creates a delightful crunch, and the slightly sweeter red onion is the perfect way to round it all off. The dill in the dressing provides the final component to this delicious, cool, refreshing salad.

4 cups chopped English cucumber
1 cup chopped red onion
1 cup roughly chopped walnuts
fresh dill fronds for garnishing

DRESSING
¼ cup roughly chopped fresh dill
¼ cup white sugar
¼ cup water
7 Tbsp white wine vinegar

1. Place the chopped cucumber and red onion in a bowl.

2. Using a hand blender, whizz the dressing ingredients and pour over the salad.

3. Chill the salad in the fridge for about an hour before serving to allow the flavours to develop.

4. When ready to serve, scatter over the walnuts and garnish with fresh dill fronds.

Spinach, Apricot and Almond

Apricots are an ancient fruit, cultivated originally in China as far back as 2000 BC. The Persians were introduced to them by traders travelling the Silk Route and they called them yellow plums or 'zardaloo'. Both apricots and almonds are members of the rose family and the nut of the apricot looks very similar to the almond, so be careful which one you eat.

⅔ cup roughly chopped dried apricots
¼ cup water if needed
3 cups baby spinach, roughly torn
½ cup flaked almonds, roasted

DRESSING
½ Tbsp orange zest
1 Tbsp orange juice
¼ cup olive oil
½ Tbsp honey
salt and pepper to taste

1. Soak the apricots in the water for about 30 minutes if they are quite dry.

2. Toss the baby spinach and apricots in a bowl.

3. Whisk the dressing ingredients, pour over the salad and toss to combine.

4. Finally, scatter over the roasted flaked almonds.

Apple, Carrot and Cabbage

When you're really busy, there's nothing easier than using ingredients that have already been prepared, like the store-bought pickled cabbage in this recipe. I love the way the ingredients all turn a delightful shade of 'pickled pink', complemented with a dash of green from the coriander. The flavours are delicious too, with the tangy, sour taste of the cabbage complementing the sweetness of the carrot and apple.

¼ cup store-bought pickled red cabbage
1 medium carrot, julienned
½ red apple, julienned with skin on
chopped fresh coriander or parsley for garnishing

DRESSING
2 Tbsp olive oil
2 Tbsp pickling juice from pickled cabbage
¼ tsp dried mixed herbs
salt and pepper to taste

1. Combine the cabbage, carrot and apple in a bowl.

2. Whisk the dressing ingredients and pour over the salad.

3. Garnish with chopped fresh coriander or parsley and serve.

This vegetarian salad collection does away with the dull and drab and instead brings a refreshing selection of healthy salads for you to enjoy. Looking after your health and getting your five-a-day really doesn't have to be a chore.

Salads are already one of the healthiest meal options to add to your diet. By adding in some extra raw fruits and vegetables, you'll be left feeling better, looking fitter, and filled with even more health and vitality. Bursting with nutrients and oh so much flavour, these recipes will not only add a burst of colour to your day-to-day eating, but plenty of nourishing goodness too.

Bring nature to the table and say hello to the reds, greens and yellows sitting in your fridge. Find a vegetarian salad to suit any occasion, from a quick side dish to add to your meal, such as the blueberry and spinach salad which is perfect for scorching-hot days, to more substantial salads that will keep you nicely nourished well into the day, such as the quinoa salad.

Vegetarian Salads

Quinoa Salad

Is quinoa (keen-wha) a grain or a seed? The debate rages, but whatever you call it, the Incas certainly knew the importance of this superfood – they called it 'the mother of all grains' and believed it was sacred. Whether you use a red, black or white variety, combined with delicious vegetarian ingredients, quinoa creates a robust salad that's perfect as a main course.

2 cups raw quinoa
½ cup vegetable stock
2 tsp olive oil
½ onion, diced
2 cups roughly chopped mixed salad leaves
1 cup diced red pepper
½ cup pitted and halved black olives
2 tomatoes, diced
½ cup shaved Parmesan

DRESSING

2 tsp onion powder
⅓ cup white wine vinegar
⅓ cup olive oil
1 tsp Dijon mustard
1 Tbsp honey
salt and pepper to taste

1. Cook the quinoa according to the packet instructions, adding the vegetable stock to provide extra flavour.

2. Heat the olive oil in a frying pan and sauté the onion until it softens and starts to brown. Set aside to cool.

3. Combine the quinoa, onion, mixed salad leaves, red pepper, olives and tomatoes in a bowl.

4. Whisk the dressing ingredients, pour over the salad and toss until well combined. Finally, scatter over the shaved Parmesan.

Tahini, Cucumber and Feta Fattouche

Fattouche is a popular Middle Eastern salad made with fried or toasted stale flatbread and various herbs and vegetables depending on the season. A traditional fattouche uses sumac, but I've mixed it up a bit by using another Middle Eastern staple, tahini, which I've added to the dressing. Tahini is a paste made from sesame seeds and olive oil, and is the perfect companion for the pita breads. All the flavours of the Middle East rolled into one salad.

2–3 pita breads
1–2 Tbsp olive oil
salt and pepper to taste
2–3 cups roughly torn cos lettuce
1 cup sliced cucumber
1 yellow pepper, cut into bite-size pieces
½ red onion, sliced
¾ cup pitted and halved black olives
2 rounds feta

DRESSING

1 Tbsp lemon juice
3 Tbsp tahini
3 Tbsp water
salt and pepper to taste

1. Preheat the oven to 180°C.

2. Place the pitas on a greased baking sheet and bake for about 5 minutes or until golden. Remove and allow to cool.

3. Break the pitas into bite-size pieces, drizzle over the olive oil and season with salt and pepper.

4. Toss the remaining ingredients, except the feta, in a bowl.

5. Whisk the dressing ingredients and pour over the salad. Toss to combine.

6. Add the pita pieces and crumble over the feta.

Mid-summer Blueberry and Spinach Salad

This is a deliciously fresh salad perfect for hot summer days and is so easy to put together. It has an unusual combination of colours, from green, red and brown to the surprise blue of the berries. The walnuts and cabbage provide the crunch, the apples and blueberries add the sweetness, while the salty feta rounds it all off.

1 red apple, finely sliced with skin on
2–3 cups loosely packed baby spinach
1 cup blueberries
½ cup roughly chopped walnuts
1 cup sliced red cabbage
⅔ cup cubed feta

DRESSING
½ cup olive oil
2 tsp wholegrain mustard
1 Tbsp sherry vinegar

1. Combine the salad ingredients in a bowl, tossing well.

2. Whisk the dressing ingredients and pour over the salad.

3. Toss well to combine and chill in the fridge before serving.

Charred Greens

Broccolini is often mistaken for young broccoli, but it's actually a hybrid of traditional broccoli and Chinese broccoli. It has smaller florets and longer, thinner stems. Although it tastes similar to normal broccoli, it's more delicate and slightly sweeter. Teamed with baby marrows and green beans, it packs a nutritional punch. Charring the greens adds a crispy, smoky flavour that pairs perfectly with the sharp Parmesan.

1 tsp olive oil
130g broccolini
200g baby marrows, sliced on the diagonal
150g fresh green beans, topped and tailed
juice and zest of 1 lemon
½ cup finely grated Parmesan
1 tsp poppy seeds

DRESSING
¼ cup olive oil
2 tsp red wine vinegar
1 tsp honey
salt and pepper to taste

1. Heat the olive oil in a frying pan and sauté all the greens for a few minutes until they start to char.

2. Transfer the vegetables to a platter and squeeze over the lemon juice and scatter over the lemon zest.

3. Whisk the dressing ingredients and pour over the vegetables. Finally, scatter over the Parmesan and poppy seeds.

Tabbouleh (Parsley, Bean and Lemon Salad)

This salad is loosely based on a classic Middle Eastern tabbouleh. The most recognisable feature of tabbouleh is that the ingredients are all finely chopped. I've substituted bulgur wheat for chickpeas and red kidney beans, but the most common ingredient, parsley, is still a prominent player. Some new introductions are feathery dill leaves and crunchy celery, while the lemon and garlic dressing rounds it off beautifully.

1 x 410g can red kidney beans, drained
  and rinsed
½ x 410g can chickpeas, drained and rinsed
1 cup cubed cucumber
¼ red onion, diced
2 stalks celery, chopped
2 cups roughly chopped fresh parsley
2 Tbsp roughly chopped fresh dill

DRESSING
¼ cup olive oil
¼ cup lemon juice
1 clove garlic, crushed
salt and pepper to taste

1. Combine the salad ingredients in a bowl and toss.

2. Whisk the dressing ingredients, pour over the salad and toss well. Chill in the fridge until ready to serve.

Shawarma Salad

This is a salad that has all the deliciousness of a classic shawarma but without the meat. One of the integral parts of a shawarma is the sauce, and this dressing hits the spot: hummus, lemon and garlic, which all blend perfectly with the chickpeas, red onion and tomato, not to mention the array of aromatic spices to complement it all. Served with pita bread on the side, you've got your Middle Eastern street food sorted.

1 tsp ground cumin
½ tsp smoked paprika
½ tsp ground turmeric
½ tsp ground cinnamon
½ tsp ground ginger
salt and pepper to taste
2 Tbsp olive oil
1 x 410g can chickpeas, rinsed and drained
2 cups chopped cucumber

2 cups chopped tomatoes
⅔ cup sliced red onion
2 cups roughly chopped fresh parsley

DRESSING
⅓ cup hummus
2 cloves garlic, crushed
2 Tbsp lemon juice
1–2 Tbsp water as needed

1. Preheat the oven to 200°C.

2. In a large bowl, mix the spices, season with salt and pepper, add the olive oil and combine to form a paste.

3. Add the chickpeas and toss through, ensuring the chickpeas are well coated. Arrange the chickpeas in a single layer on a greased baking sheet and bake for 15–20 minutes until crispy. Remove and allow to cool.

4. Combine the balance of the salad ingredients in a serving bowl, add the chickpeas and toss to combine.

5. Whisk the dressing ingredients and drizzle over the salad.

Honey-mustard Aubergine Salad

Filling, flavourful and creamy are brought together in this tantalising salad. Emulsifying the oil with the honey and mustard creates the smooth and creamy texture of the dressing. Whether you call them aubergines, brinjals or eggplants, they're a worthy addition to vegetarian salads, as they're quite substantial and meaty. The heady aroma is from the dill and mint, and to complete the dish, the tangy pomegranate arils provide a burst of colour.

1–2 medium aubergines
2 tsp olive oil
½ red onion, sliced
2 cups mixed salad leaves or baby spinach
2–3 rounds feta
¼ cup roughly chopped fresh dill
¼ cup roughly chopped fresh mint
¼ cup pomegranate arils

DRESSING
⅓ cup olive oil
3 Tbsp lemon juice
1 Tbsp honey
1 tsp Dijon mustard
salt and pepper to tast

1. Slice the aubergines lengthways, 0.5–1cm thick.

2. Heat the olive oil in a frying pan and gently fry the aubergines and red onion until softened. Remove and allow to cool.

3. Place the mixed salad leaves or baby spinach on a platter and place the aubergines and onion on top. Crumble over the feta.

4. Scatter over the dill, mint and pomegranate arils.

5. Whisk the dressing ingredients and pour over the salad.

Cheesy Roast Vegetable Salad

Cheese makes everything taste better. Nothing could be more appetising than chargrilled halloumi draped over vegetables that have just started to char and caramelise. Dry-grilling halloumi creates a most appealing golden crust with a soft and squishy inside. The citrus dressing pulls together this salad brimming with vegetable goodness, creating a substantial side or main that is guaranteed to become a regular feature on your table.

1–2 medium aubergines, sliced lengthways about 1cm thick
1½ cups diagonally sliced baby marrow
2 cups quartered red pepper
2 cups cubed butternut
¼ cup olive oil
2 cloves garlic, crushed
½ tsp dried rosemary
salt and pepper to taste
300g halloumi, cut into 0.5cm slices

2 cups roughly torn baby spinach
½ cup pitted black olives
fresh thyme sprigs for garnishing

DRESSING
¼ cup orange juice
¼ cup olive oil
2 tsp white wine vinegar
salt and pepper to taste

1. Preheat the oven to 180°C.

2. Place the aubergine slices, baby marrow, red pepper and butternut on a greased baking sheet.

3. Whisk the olive oil, garlic, rosemary, salt and pepper and pour over the vegetables. Toss to combine and roast for 20–30 minutes until the butternut has softened and the vegetables start to char. Remove and set aside.

4. In a non-stick griddle pan, cook the halloumi until grill lines appear.

5. Place the baby spinach leaves on a platter, arrange the vegetables on top, drape over the halloumi slices and scatter over the black olives.

6. Whisk the dressing ingredients and pour over the salad. Finish it off with a few sprigs of fresh thyme.

Breakfast Salad

I can hear you thinking: a breakfast salad? Well, why not? Whether you eat this at breakfast or later in the day, you'll be getting a healthy dose of greens, fibre and protein. And it's colourful, too! I enjoy the addition of salty feta and spicy harissa paste to round it all off. Whether you like your eggs poached or boiled, this unusual salad is sure to be a winner.

360g butternut, cubed
4–8 eggs
2 tsp butter
1 cup quartered portobellini mushrooms
salt and pepper to taste
1 x 410g can chickpeas, drained and rinsed
1 tsp paprika

2–3 tsp olive oil
4 tsp harissa paste
1 cup watercress
2 cups baby spinach
1 cup cubed feta
a few slices toasted ciabatta for serving

1. Cook the butternut in a saucepan of boiling water for about 15 minutes or until just tender. Drain and set aside.

2. Depending on your preference, either poach or boil one or more eggs per person.

3. Melt the butter in a hot frying pan and sauté the mushrooms until golden. Season with salt and pepper, remove from the pan and set aside.

4. Season the chickpeas with the paprika and some salt and pepper. In the same pan you used for the mushrooms, sauté the chickpeas until they start to crisp. Remove from the pan and set aside.

5. Add some olive oil to the pan and sauté the parboiled butternut until it starts to char.

6. Smear a teaspoon of harissa paste on each serving plate and arrange the watercress and baby spinach on top. Add the butternut, feta and mushrooms. Top with the cooked eggs and serve with toasted ciabatta on the side.

Grilled Vegetable Stacks

I love the idea of stacking the vegetables instead of serving them tossed together. The best part, though, is the melting goat's cheese on top. It makes eating all these vegetables worthwhile. The dash of sweetness from the balsamic reduction will make you forget you're getting your five-a-day dose of goodness.

1–2 aubergines, thickly sliced (you'll need 8 slices)
70g fresh green beans, topped and tailed
1–2 red onions, thickly sliced
2 carrots, cut into batons
2 red peppers, cut into chunks
6 baby corn, halved lengthways

1 cup cherry tomatoes
3 Tbsp olive oil
1 clove garlic, crushed
salt and pepper to taste
150g goat's cheese, sliced
3 Tbsp breadcrumbs
balsamic vinegar reduction for drizzling

1. Preheat the oven's grill.

2. Grease a baking sheet and place all the vegetables, except the cherry tomatoes, in a single layer, keeping them separate. Leave space for the tomatoes to be added later.

3. Mix the olive oil, garlic, salt and pepper and pour over the vegetables.

4. Place under the grill for about 7 minutes and then add the cherry tomatoes. Continue to grill until all the vegetables start to soften and char.

5. Roll the goat's cheese slices in the breadcrumbs, place on a separate baking sheet and grill until the cheese just starts to melt. Remove and set aside.

6. To assemble the stacks, place an aubergine slice on the bottom, add some green beans, red onions and carrots, followed by another slice of aubergine and then the red peppers, baby corn and cherry tomatoes.

7. Place the melted goat's cheese slices on top and drizzle over some balsamic vinegar reduction.

Robot Pepper and Caper Salad

Super easy, quick and healthy, this is the ideal salad to pull together at the drop of a hat. It's sweet, sharp and full of colour. Bell peppers are often called robot peppers because of their colours, which are reminiscent of traffic lights, known in South Africa as robots. A red pepper is simply a ripened green pepper, which makes it the sweetest of the three.

1 red pepper
1 green pepper
1 yellow pepper
4 tsp capers
1–2 cups torn and loosely packed baby spinach

DRESSING
8 tsp olive oil
8 tsp orange juice
4 tsp sherry vinegar
salt and pepper to taste

1. Julienne the peppers and roughly chop the capers.

2. Mix with the spinach in a serving bowl.

3. Whisk the dressing ingredients, pour over the salad and toss to combine.

Moroccan Cauliflower Salad

The heavily aromatic spice cumin is synonymous with Morocco, as are Medjool dates. I like using the dried version of the dates, as they're not dehydrated, which makes them soft and sticky. As they dry, their sugars become more concentrated, making them sweeter. This Moroccan dynamic duo of dates and cumin is just what the cauliflower needs to create a dish that is reminiscent of the spice markets of Marrakesh and Casablanca, filled as they are with large, colourful and fragrant sacks of spices.

1 head cauliflower
1 Tbsp olive oil
4 spring onions, finely sliced
1 clove garlic, finely chopped
¼ cup chopped dried Medjool dates
½ tsp ground cumin
½ cup roughly chopped fresh parsley

½ cup roughly chopped fresh mint
¼ cup pomegranate arils

DRESSING
¼ cup tahini
3 Tbsp lemon juice
2 Tbsp water

1. Break the cauliflower into florets and chop into bite-size pieces.

2. Heat the olive oil in a frying pan and gently fry the spring onions and garlic for about 1 minute.

3. Add the cauliflower, dates and cumin and continue to cook for 3–4 minutes. Remove the pan from the heat.

4. Whisk the dressing ingredients and pour over the cauliflower. Toss until well combined.

5. Mix through half the parsley, mint and pomegranate arils.

6. Transfer the salad to a serving bowl and scatter over the remaining parsley, mint and pomegranate arils.

Papaya, Black Bean and Avo Ensemble

Black turtle beans, so-called because of their hard-looking shells, have a mild sweet flavour and somewhat creamy texture. More often referred to simply as black beans, these have been eaten in North America for around 7 000 years. They're very healthy, because they're big on nutrients and low on fat and sugar. Their dark colour contrasts beautifully with the orange of the papaya and the green tinges of the avocado, making this salad a feast for the eyes, too.

1 x 410g can black beans, drained and rinsed
1 cup chopped papaya
⅔ cup halved cherry tomatoes
1 medium avocado, diced
½ red onion, finely sliced
juice of 2 oranges

juice of 1 lemon
2 Tbsp chopped fresh coriander
salt and pepper to taste

1. Place the black beans, papaya, tomatoes, avocado and onion in a serving bowl.

2. Squeeze over the orange and lemon juices and scatter over the fresh coriander.

3. Season with salt and pepper and toss until well combined.

The Kyoto Salad
(Edamame, Mango and Chickpea Salad)

Eh-dah-mah-meh, which means 'beans on branches' in Japanese, is a variety of the common soybean. Soya is a good source of protein and provides a healthy dose of fats and carbohydrates. In fact, this salad is packed with protein, as the chickpeas are also protein rich. The mango brings some sweetness, while the cucumber creates the freshness, making this the ideal salad to have on hot summer days.

1 cup shelled edamame beans
1 cup canned chickpeas, drained and rinsed
½ cup diced mango
½ cup diced cucumber
2 Tbsp diced red onion
salt and pepper to taste
black sesame seeds and microherbs
   for garnishing

DRESSING
2 Tbsp olive oil
2 tsp red wine vinegar
2 tsp lemon juice
½ tsp crushed garlic

1. Cook the edamame beans according to the packet instructions.

2. Mix the salad ingredients in a bowl and season generously with salt and pepper.

3. Whisk the dressing ingredients, pour over the salad and toss gently to combine.

4. Chill in the fridge. When ready to serve, garnish with black sesame seeds and microherbs.

Thai Tofu and Noodle Salad

For me, Thai cuisine is synonymous with spicy, and this salad is no exception. Even the noodles and tofu remind me of the bustling streets of Bangkok. Tofu is a good source of protein and is remarkably low in calories, while still providing your body with all the amino acids it needs. It's perfect for adding to salads and, because of its texture, it easily absorbs the flavours of the dressing. The bean sprouts bring the last bit of Asian zing to this tasty salad.

100g tofu, cut into bite-size pieces
1 Tbsp olive oil
60g thin egg noodles
1 cup torn baby spinach
½ red pepper, julienned
1 large carrot, julienned
2 spring onions, sliced on the diagonal
2 baby marrows, julienned
1 Tbsp roughly chopped fresh mint
1 Tbsp roughly chopped fresh basil
½ cup bean sprouts

DRESSING
2 Tbsp olive oil
1 Tbsp fish sauce
½ tsp crushed garlic
2 Tbsp lime juice
1 Tbsp brown sugar
1 Tbsp sesame oil
1–2 tsp sriracha (depending on how hot you like it)

1. Preheat the oven to 200°C.

2. Place the tofu on a greased baking sheet and drizzle over the olive oil, ensuring the tofu is well coated. Bake for about 20 minutes or until browned, tossing halfway.

3. Cook the egg noodles according to the packet instructions.

4. Combine the remaining salad ingredients, except the bean sprouts, in a bowl and toss with the noodles.

5. Transfer to a serving a platter and scatter over the browned tofu.

6. Whisk the dressing ingredients and pour over the salad. Toss to coat and garnish with the bean sprouts.

Zingy Roast Carrot Salad

It's common knowledge that eating carrots will improve your eyesight, but there are many other benefits, too. They've been linked to boosting the immune system, reducing cholesterol and controlling blood pressure. Best of all, roasting them concentrates their flavour, turning them golden and caramelising their edges. Just don't overdo your carrot consumption, as eating too many of them can turn your skin an orange-yellow colour, but luckily only temporarily.

400g carrots
¼ cup olive oil
2 Tbsp harissa paste
2 Tbsp lemon juice
dried chilli flakes for garnishing (optional)
3 Tbsp chopped fresh parsley

DRESSING
¼ cup olive oil
zest of 2 lemons
1 Tbsp lemon juice
2 Tbsp orange juice
2 tsp harissa paste

1. Preheat the oven to 190°C.

2. Slice the carrots lengthways into strips and place in a single layer on a greased baking sheet.

3. Combine the olive oil, harissa paste and lemon juice and pour over the carrots. Toss well to coat.

4. Bake for 10 minutes, tossing halfway, until the carrots have softened and started to char. Transfer to a serving dish.

5. Whisk the dressing ingredients and pour over the carrots. Garnish with chilli flakes if using and finish it off with the chopped fresh parsley.

Sesame-dressed Black Bean and Lentil Salad

Sriracha is generally made from chilli peppers, garlic, vinegar and salt. It's still debatable where exactly this sauce originated, but the popular belief is that it was invented by a Thai lady who lived in the Thai town of Si Racha. What isn't debatable is that it's a delicious, spicy sauce that works extremely well as part of this Asian-style dressing.

½ x 410g can brown lentils, drained and rinsed
1 x 410g can black beans, drained and rinsed
1 red pepper, diced
½ small red onion, diced
1 large tomato, diced
1 cup roughly chopped fresh coriander

DRESSING
1 Tbsp soy sauce
3 Tbsp olive oil
1 Tbsp rice wine vinegar
½ Tbsp sesame oil
½ Tbsp lemon juice
1 Tbsp honey
¼ tsp crushed garlic
¼ tsp grated fresh ginger
½–1 tsp sriracha (depending on how hot you like it)
1 Tbsp water

1. Place the lentils, black beans, red pepper, red onion and tomato in a large bowl and toss.

2. Whisk the dressing ingredients until thoroughly mixed, pour over the salad and toss to combine.

3. Scatter over the chopped fresh coriander and serve.

Raw Pumpkin Surprise

Pumpkin is a nutritious vegetable, bursting with phytochemicals and vitamins that protect the body against carcinogens and boost the immune system. Eating it raw is more unusual but no less appetising. Soaking it in the sauce softens it, and the seeds add a tantalising crunch and an additional punch of healthy goodness.

2 tsp minced fresh chilli	3 cups julienned pumpkin
1 tsp crushed garlic	1½ rounds feta, cut into chunks
⅓ cup orange juice	3 Tbsp raisins
1½ Tbsp white wine vinegar	3 Tbsp pumpkin seeds, toasted
2½ Tbsp olive oil	5 tsp orange zest
1 tsp salt	dried chilli flakes for garnishing

1. Combine the minced chilli, garlic, orange juice, white wine vinegar, olive oil and salt in a large bowl.

2. Add the pumpkin and toss to coat. Leave to soften for about 15 minutes.

3. Drain any excess liquid from the pumpkin and add the feta, raisins, toasted pumpkin seeds and orange zest.

4. Toss to combine, transfer to a serving dish and garnish with chilli flakes.

Cauliflower Floret Salad

This salad has many of the elements you'd associate with a potato salad, but I've used cauliflower florets instead of potatoes. The celery provides a tantalising crunch, while the crispy capers and boiled eggs are quintessential partners in a potato salad. It wouldn't be a 'potato salad' if it didn't have a creamy dressing, and this is no exception. To add a bit of oomph, I've added apple cider vinegar and a dose of Dijon mustard.

	DRESSING
4 cups cauliflower florets	½ cup light mayonnaise
¼ cup capers	4 tsp apple cider vinegar
2 Tbsp olive oil	2 Tbsp Dijon mustard
3 hard-boiled eggs, chopped	1 tsp garlic powder
1 small onion, finely sliced	1 tsp paprika
3 stalks celery, sliced	4 tsp water
salt and pepper to taste	salt and pepper to taste
¼ cup chopped chives	

1. Bring a saucepan of salted water to the boil and simmer the cauliflower florets for 5 minutes until tender. Drain well.

2. Rinse the capers under cold water to remove excess salt, then dry thoroughly on paper towel.

3. In a small saucepan, sauté the capers in the olive oil for 3–5 minutes, stirring occasionally, until brown and crispy. Once cooked, remove with a slotted spoon and drain on paper towel.

4. Gently toss together the cauliflower, eggs, onion and celery in a serving bowl.

5. Whisk the dressing ingredients, pour over the salad and toss gently to coat.

6. Season generously with salt and pepper, and garnish with the crispy capers and chopped chives.

Pizza Salad

Pita breads are so versatile. Here, halved through the middle, they make perfect thin pizza bases. To add a spicy zing, I spread harissa paste over the bases instead of the classic tomato paste. And it wouldn't be a pizza without melted mozzarella, but to up the game a bit, I use buffalo mozzarella, which gives a creaminess you don't often associate with pizza. Once you've had one, you'll be reaching for one more.

½ cup olive oil, plus extra for drizzling
1 Tbsp harissa paste
1 clove garlic, crushed
2–3 pita breads, halved through the middle
140g buffalo mozzarella
1 cup sliced rosa tomatoes

½ cup loosely packed rocket
1 cup loosely packed watercress
½ cup loosely packed baby spinach
½ cup bean sprouts
¼ cup pumpkin seeds, toasted
salt and pepper to taste

1. Preheat the oven to 200°C.

2. In a jug, whisk the olive oil, harissa paste and garlic.

3. Place the halved pita breads on a greased baking sheet and brush with three-quarters of the harissa oil.

4. Break the buffalo mozzarella into pieces and scatter over the pita breads, along with the rosa tomatoes.

5. Bake for 5–7 minutes until the pita breads start to crisp and the mozzarella starts to melt.

6. Remove from the oven, drizzle over the remaining harissa oil and scatter over the rocket, watercress, baby spinach, bean sprouts and toasted pumpkin seeds.

7. Season generously with salt and pepper and drizzle over some extra olive oil. Serve immediately.

What better way to incorporate the piquant taste of the sea into your eating regime than with a stunning contemporary seafood salad. This recipe collection combines the alluring, delicate flavours of the ocean with the crisp, clear flavours of the garden to bring you a wide variety of delectable salads that are sure to impress.

Salads are the perfect fix when you're craving something fresh and healthy, and when it comes to eating healthily, seafood is an excellent source of protein. The ocean's bounty is abundant in proteins, nutrients, omega-3 fatty acids and vitamins, making a scrumptious seafood salad the intelligent option for those looking for a meal that's diet friendly and loaded with nutrients. Just be sure to source your fish and seafood from reputable suppliers to ensure the sustainability of the species.

Whether you have a hankering for something light and breezy, such as a smoked salmon citrus salad, or want to really impress with something truly memorable, such as an exotic crayfish salad, there's a recipe here for you. This collection of seafaring salads offers lovely, simple lunches, dinners or anytime snacks, as well as dishes that will shine and add elegance to the table when you want to impress.

Fish & Seafood Salads

Prawn Caesar Salad

This fresh and tantalising salad has all the components you associate with a classic Caesar salad, and then some. Anchovy, egg, Parmesan, and the inimitable cos lettuce to provide that classic crunch are elevated with the addition of marinated prawns, which will have your friends coming back time and again.

600–700g prawns, deveined and shelled
4 rashers bacon
2 tsp olive oil
4 cups cos lettuce leaves
½ cup shaved Parmesan
2 hard-boiled eggs, roughly chopped

MARINADE
1 Tbsp lemon juice
2–3 cloves garlic, finely chopped
2 Tbsp olive oil
salt and pepper to taste

DRESSING
3 Tbsp tangy light mayonnaise
1 Tbsp water
2 Tbsp olive oil
1 clove garlic
1 anchovy fillet
1 Tbsp lemon juice
3 Tbsp grated Parmesan

1. Combine the marinade ingredients and pour into a flat, shallow dish. Add the prawns, toss to combine and marinate for about 10 minutes.

2. Heat a non-stick frying pan and fry the bacon until crispy. Remove the bacon, break into bits and set aside.

3. Whizz the dressing ingredients using a hand blender and keep in the fridge until ready to use.

4. Wipe the frying pan, add the olive oil and fry the prawns until they turn pink and are cooked through.

5. To assemble the salad, arrange the cos lettuce leaves on a platter, scatter over the bacon bits, place the prawns on top and drizzle over the dressing. Finally, scatter over the Parmesan and chopped eggs.

Sesame Salmon Salad

Pan-searing is my favourite way to cook salmon. It's crispy on the outside while tender, soft and flaky on the inside. It's also super quick to do. Black sesame seeds provide the wow factor, making this a showstopper of a salad. The sneaky addition of basil pesto in the dressing provides an additional flavour bomb of garlicky basil goodness. This colourful, healthy salad bursting with contrasting flavours and textures is sure to become a regular treat at your table.

2 Tbsp olive oil
4 salmon fillets, skin removed
2–3 Tbsp black sesame seeds
1 red pepper, julienned
1 yellow pepper, julienned
½ red onion, sliced
1 avocado, sliced
fresh parsley or microgreens for garnishing

DRESSING
½ Tbsp basil pesto
1 tsp lemon juice
¼ cup olive oil
salt and pepper to taste

1. Heat the olive oil in a frying or griddle pan until hot. Sear the salmon fillets until cooked to your liking. I prefer my salmon quite pink.

2. Pour the sesame seeds onto a plate and press the salmon fillets into them to coat. Set the fillets aside.

3. Place the red and yellow peppers, onion and avocado on a platter and position the salmon fillets on top.

4. Whisk the dressing ingredients and drizzle over the salad. Garnish with fresh parsley or microgreens.

Eastern Prawn and Asparagus Salad

Lemon and seafood are a match made in heaven. The other perfect match is dill and seafood. This salad has them both. Marinating the prawns while you prepare the rest of the salad will give them just enough time to take on the marinade's flavours, providing them with a piquancy reminiscent of the exotic East.

500–600g prawns, deveined and shelled,
   tails intact
3 Tbsp butter
340g fresh baby asparagus spears, sliced on
   the diagonal
3 Tbsp lemon juice
2 cups sugar snap peas, sliced on the diagonal
3 spring onions, sliced on the diagonal
3 Tbsp roughly chopped fresh dill
3 Tbsp slivered almonds, roasted

MARINADE
¼ cup soy sauce
¼ cup oyster sauce
1 Tbsp fish sauce
1 Tbsp honey
1 Tbsp lemon juice
1 clove garlic, crushed

DRESSING
3 Tbsp olive oil
2 Tbsp lemon juice
½ tsp Dijon mustard
salt and pepper to taste

1. Whisk the marinade ingredients, pour into a shallow bowl and add the prawns. Toss the prawns in the marinade to ensure they are well coated, then set aside to marinate while you cook the asparagus.

2. Melt half the butter in a frying pan and sauté the asparagus until just charred. Remove from the pan and set aside.

3. Melt the remaining butter in the same pan and add the prawns. Cook until the prawns are pink on both sides. Remove from the heat, drizzle over the lemon juice and set aside.

4. Whisk the dressing ingredients and set aside.

5. To serve, place the asparagus on a platter, scatter over the sugar snap peas and spring onions and place the prawns on top. Pour over the dressing and scatter over the fresh dill and roasted slivered almonds.

Scandi-style Salmon and Potato Salad

New (or baby) potatoes are really the star attraction here. In Norway, new potatoes are so important that the first crops are actually taken to the Royal Palace. They are reminiscent of summer, which is so short in the north. In keeping with the Scandi theme, I've included salmon to rest amiably among the potatoes. The creamy mustard sauce with bright fresh dill completes this appetising salad.

500–600g Norwegian salmon fillets,
   skin removed
salt and pepper to taste
1 lemon, sliced
6–8 new potatoes
1 cup sliced celery
½ cup finely sliced red onion

SAUCE
¼ cup finely chopped fresh dill
¼ cup finely chopped fresh parsley
2 tsp Dijon mustard
2 Tbsp lemon juice
½ cup double-cream plain yoghurt
zest of 2 lemons
juice of 1 lemon

1. Preheat the oven to 200°C.

2. Place the salmon fillets on a greased baking sheet and season generously with salt and pepper. Place the lemon slices on top of the fillets and bake for about 15 minutes until cooked to preference.

3. Bring a saucepan of salted water to the boil and cook the new potatoes in their skins.

4. To assemble the salad, halve the new potatoes and place on a platter along with the celery and red onion.

5. Flake the salmon fillets and scatter over the vegetables.

6. Whisk the sauce ingredients and dollop on top.

Punchy Tuna Pasta Salad

Pasta salads are always popular but not always that healthy, drowning in heavy cream or mayonnaise. But this salad is overflowing with goodness without sacrificing any flavour. Fresh tuna is a health powerhouse, being a source of high-quality protein with almost no fat. Even pasta can be part of a well-balanced diet if eaten in moderation, providing the body with necessary energy. Tomatoes also have a beneficial role to play here, being an excellent source of the antioxidant lycopene. All good and healthy reasons to tuck in.

400–500g tuna steaks
210g penne pasta
¼ cup olive oil
2 cups small mixed tomatoes, halved depending
   on size
1 cup pitted and halved black olives
2 cups loosely packed rocket
1 cup roughly torn baby spinach
2 Tbsp lemon juice
salt and pepper to taste

MARINADE
½ cup white wine
2 tsp lemon zest
1 clove garlic, crushed
1 tsp fennel seeds, crushed
2 Tbsp olive oil
salt and pepper to taste

DRESSING
2 Tbsp roughly chopped capers
2 Tbsp lemon juice
2 tsp Dijon mustard
2 Tbsp olive oil

1. Whisk the marinade ingredients, pour into a shallow bowl and add the tuna steaks. Leave to marinate in the fridge for 30–60 minutes, turning once or twice to ensure both sides are covered.

2. Cook the pasta according to the packet instructions.

3. Heat half the olive oil in a frying or griddle pan until hot and then sear the tuna steaks on both sides. Pour in some of the used marinade and continue to cook until the tuna is done to your liking. I prefer mine rare.

4. Toss the pasta, tomatoes, olives, rocket and baby spinach in a bowl. Whisk the dressing ingredients, pour over and toss to combine. Transfer to a serving platter.

5. Slice the tuna steaks about 1cm thick and place on top of the salad.

6. Drizzle over the remaining olive oil and the lemon juice, and season generously with salt and pepper.

Saucy Scallop Salad

Scallops are a highly prized shellfish known for their delicate taste and texture. They're deliciously sweet and tender and melt in your mouth. They're surprisingly rich, so only a few per plate will turn your salad into a filling delicacy. This is just as well, as they can be rather pricy. The dressing is inspired by the classic French velouté sauce. Velouté means 'velvety', which is an accurate description of this creamy dressing.

1 cup uncooked couscous
2 Tbsp fish stock concentrate
2 cups warm water
¼ cup finely chopped fresh parsley
¼ cup finely chopped fresh dill
2 tsp butter
12 scallops
salt and pepper to taste
2 tsp lemon juice
2–3 cups sliced cos lettuce
fresh dill fronds for garnishing
lemon wedges for garnishing

SAUCE
50g butter
1 onion, finely chopped
200ml dry white wine
1 tsp fish stock concentrate
¼ cup water
¼ cup finely chopped fresh mixed herbs
1 tsp lemon juice
1 tsp lemon zest
150ml cream

1. Begin by making the sauce. Melt 25g butter in a frying pan, add the onion and cook for about 5 minutes.

2. Add the wine and cook until reduced by half, then mix in the fish stock concentrate, water, fresh herbs, lemon juice and lemon zest and continue to reduce for about 15 minutes.

3. Add the cream and continue to reduce. Finally, add the remaining butter, allow to melt and then stir through. Remove from the heat and allow to cool completely. The sauce should thicken as it cools.

4. Place the couscous, fish stock concentrate and warm water in a bowl, cover and set aside until the couscous has absorbed all the liquid. Fluff with a fork, then stir through the fresh parsley and dill.

5. Melt the butter in a hot frying pan and season the scallops with salt and pepper. Add the scallops and lemon juice to the pan and sear the scallops on both sides, being careful not to overcook them.

6. Place the cos lettuce on a serving plate. Scatter over the couscous and top with the scallops.

7. Pour over the sauce and garnish with fresh dill fronds and lemon wedges. Serve immediately.

Spicy Calamari Salad

Calamari is the Italian word for squid, and this mollusc, found all over the world, is a seafood staple in many countries. It's a regular feature in salads in Greece and a common street food in Asia. It's a versatile protein with a mild flavour that cooks quickly and works well in a wide variety of dishes. I like to marinate calamari, as it easily absorbs spices and aromas, creating an array of different flavours.

500g calamari tubes
1 red pepper, halved
1 cup chopped small mixed tomatoes
1 avocado, chopped
2 Tbsp finely chopped red onion
2 Tbsp olive oil
2 Tbsp lemon juice
2 tsp lemon pepper
salt to taste

¼ cup finely chopped fresh mint
2 Tbsp finely chopped fresh dill

MARINADE
2 tsp minced fresh red chilli
1 tsp crushed garlic
2 tsp lemon juice
2 tsp olive oil
2 tsp white wine

1. Preheat the oven 200°C.

2. Whisk the marinade ingredients in a shallow bowl, add the calamari tubes and marinate for about 30 minutes.

3. Place the red pepper halves cut-side down on a greased baking sheet and roast for 15–20 minutes until the skins are charred. Allow to cool slightly, then remove the skins and chop the flesh.

4. Toss the tomatoes, avocado, red pepper and red onion in a bowl. Combine the olive oil, lemon juice, lemon pepper and salt and pour over the salad mixture. Toss well.

5. Sauté the calamari in a hot non-stick frying pan for 3–4 minutes until cooked. Be careful not to overcook the calamari, as the tubes will become rubbery.

6. Place the salad mixture onto a serving platter, add the calamari tubes and scatter over the fresh mint and dill.

Exotic Crayfish Stack

The scene is set, the table is under the trees, lit by dappled sunlight and beautifully laid with crisp white linen, glistening crystalware and vases overflowing with summer flowers. All that remains is to impress your guests with crayfish tails to round off your stylish menu. There are a surprising number of ingredients here, but don't worry, they all come together remarkably quickly, which means you'll have this elegant salad on your table in no time at all. Served with an ice-cold glass of pink bubbles, your guests will be bowled over.

¼ cup olive oil
4 tsp Tabasco sauce
¼ cup lemon juice
2 tsp chopped fresh fennel
2 tsp chopped fresh parsley
salt and pepper to taste
4–6 crayfish tails
12 large mixed salad leaves
1 cup cucumber ribbons
1 mango, sliced
1 avocado, sliced (optional)

DRESSING
¼ cup lime juice
½ Tbsp lime zest
¼ cup red wine vinegar
1 Tbsp soy sauce
1 Tbsp honey
½ cup olive oil
1 clove garlic, crushed
½ tsp finely chopped fresh chilli
1 tsp ground cumin
salt to taste

1. Preheat the oven to 180°C.

2. Mix the olive oil, Tabasco sauce, lemon juice, fennel, parsley, salt and pepper.

3. Place the crayfish tails in a roasting pan and liberally brush the fleshy part of each with the flavoured oil. Bake for about 10 minutes until just cooked.

4. Place the mixed salad leaves on a platter and drape over the cucumber ribbons. Scatter over the mango and avocado slices, if using.

5. Whizz all the dressing ingredients using a hand blender and pour over the salad.

6. Finally, top with the crayfish tails and drizzle over any pan juices. Serve immediately.

Tuna Tartare Salad

Tartare is traditionally prepared with beef, but I've used tuna here. It's best to use the finest, freshest quality tuna you can find because the fish isn't cooked. Topped off with delicate quail eggs and a tangy, creamy dressing, this elegant dish also works well as an appetiser and is a sure way to impress your guests.

500g tuna steaks, diced
½ cup diced cucumber
4 tsp diced red onion
4 tsp olive oil
2 tsp white balsamic vinegar
salt and pepper to taste
1 avocado, thinly sliced
4 quail eggs, cooked and sliced in half
a few slices toasted ciabatta for serving
lemon wedges for serving

DRESSING

3 cloves garlic
4 anchovy fillets
¼ cup tangy light mayonnaise
¼ cup sour cream
2 Tbsp water

1. Mix the tuna, cucumber and red onion in a bowl. Pour over the olive oil and balsamic vinegar and season with salt and pepper. Toss to combine and place in the fridge to chill.

2. Whizz the dressing ingredients using a hand blender.

3. Plate individually or as a platter. Place the tuna tartare on the bottom and drape with the avocado slices. Top with the quail eggs and drizzle over the dressing.

4. Serve with toasted ciabatta and lemon wedges on the side.

Sweet and Sour Oyster Salad

Oysters are eaten in myriad ways. Sure, there's the customary lemon with a dash of Tabasco, or the classic oysters Rockefeller. But the world is your oyster, so how about trying this unexpected version with a sweet and sour salad on top? The salty, sodium-rich flavour of the oysters partners perfectly with this tangy Asian-style sauce. You'll certainly surprise your guests with this memorable dish.

1 Tbsp olive oil
¼ cup chopped red onion
¼ red pepper, diced
¼ green pepper, diced
8 oysters in their half shells, membranes removed
2 tsp lemon juice
3–4 cos lettuce leaves, finely sliced
2 Tbsp diced mango
fresh coriander for garnishing
dried chilli flakes for garnishing

SAUCE

2 tsp cornflour
5 Tbsp water
1 Tbsp white sugar
1 Tbsp white wine vinegar
1 Tbsp soy sauce
salt and pepper to taste

1. Heat the olive oil in a frying pan and gently sauté the onion and peppers until softened. Set aside to cool.

2. To make the sauce, mix the cornflour with a touch of the water to form a paste. In a saucepan over low heat, combine the remaining sauce ingredients along with the rest of the water and the cornflour paste. Stir until the sauce thickens, then stir in the onion and peppers.

3. Drizzle each oyster in its half shell with ¼ tsp lemon juice.

4. Spoon some sauce on top of each oyster, scatter over some sliced lettuce, add a few diced mango pieces, and garnish with fresh coriander and dried chilli flakes.

Pickled and Spiced Fish Salad

Being born in Cape Town, I have fond memories of eating pickled fish, as it was a regular fixture on my ouma's menu. This dish is very popular in Malay culture and is eaten especially over Easter, but no one knows its exact origins. I like the theory that it was created by the Cape Malay fishermen in an attempt to preserve their catch. This is an adaptation of my own family recipe handed down to me by my ouma.

¼ cup cake flour
salt and pepper to taste
400–500g hake portions, skin removed
¼ cup olive oil
1 white onion, sliced
1 tsp crushed garlic
20 black peppercorns
2 bay leaves
1½ cups white wine vinegar
1 cup water
⅔–1 cup brown sugar
1 Tbsp medium curry powder
1 tsp ground turmeric
1 tsp ground cumin

1 tsp ground coriander
6–8 baby potatoes
2 baby fennel bulbs, sliced
½ medium red onion, thinly sliced
2 Tbsp chopped sundried tomatoes
8–10 cos lettuce leaves
fresh parsley for garnishing

DRESSING
¼ cup olive oil
2 Tbsp lemon juice
1 tsp Dijon mustard
2½ Tbsp sour cream
salt and pepper to taste

1. Season the flour with salt and pepper and coat the hake.

2. Heat half the olive oil in a large, deep frying pan and cook the fish for 4–5 minutes per side until golden and cooked through. Remove the fish from the pan and set aside.

3. Add the remaining olive oil to the same pan and cook the white onion and garlic until the onion has softened.

4. Add the black peppercorns, bay leaves, white wine vinegar, water and sugar and bring to the boil. Boil until the sugar has dissolved.

5. Add the curry powder, turmeric, cumin and coriander, season with salt and stir until well combined.

6. Lay the fish in a dish and pour over the spiced pickling sauce, ensuring the fish is well coated. Allow to cool before covering, then place in the fridge for at least 24 hours to allow the flavours to develop.

7. Gently boil the baby potatoes in their skins in a saucepan of salted water until soft. Drain and allow to cool before cutting into bite-size pieces.

8. Once cooled, mix the potatoes in a bowl with the fennel, red onion and sundried tomatoes.

9. Whisk the dressing ingredients and pour over the salad, tossing to ensure everything is well coated.

10. Remove the fish from the fridge and slice into bite-size pieces.

11. Place the cos lettuce leaves on a platter and put 1–2 Tbsp of salad into each one. Place some pickled fish on top and garnish with fresh parsley.

Shiitake and Kingklip Salad

Shiitake mushrooms have a strong, earthy flavour and full of umami. They have brown, umbrella-like caps and tan stems with off-white gills. When cooked, they take on a deliciously velvety and meaty texture. They're a bewitching partner to the za'atar-spiced kingklip, blending the flavours of Asia with the Middle East, where za'atar is a popular spice. The addition of generous amounts of coriander provides a citrusy and tart flavour to complete this simple yet exotic salad.

1 tsp dried thyme
1 tsp za'atar spice
salt and pepper to taste
350–450g kingklip, cubed
1 Tbsp olive oil
1 Tbsp lemon juice
2–3 Tbsp butter
5–6 cups shiitake mushrooms, sliced
1½ cups chopped fresh coriander
1½ cups torn mixed salad leaves
3–4 Tbsp diagonally sliced spring onion

DRESSING
2 tsp honey
2 Tbsp olive oil
1 Tbsp lemon juice
salt and pepper to taste

1. Combine the thyme, za'atar spice, salt and pepper in a shallow, flat bowl. Add the kingklip and toss until well coated.

2. Heat the olive oil in a frying pan and sauté the kingklip cubes until cooked. Remove the kingklip from the pan, drizzle over the lemon juice and set aside.

3. Add the butter to the same pan and sauté the mushrooms until golden.

4. Place the coriander and mixed salad leaves on a serving plate and scatter over the spring onion, mushrooms and kingklip.

5. Whisk the dressing ingredients, pour over the salad and toss to combine.

Smoked Trout and Tahini Salad

Do you get that sinking feeling when guests unexpectedly decide to stay and you have to serve them something to eat? No need to panic – this salad is a winner and you'll have it on the table faster than you can order pizza. It's healthy, too. Trout, whether smoked or fresh, is a powerhouse of protein, loaded with omega 3s and bursting with vitamin B. You can be sure you're serving your guests a colourful salad full of goodness.

1 cup shredded red cabbage
1 cup shredded cos lettuce
1 medium carrot, julienned
200–300g smoked trout ribbons
2 spring onions, sliced on the diagonal
2 Tbsp roughly chopped fresh coriander
2 tsp black or toasted white sesame seeds
lemon wedges for serving

DRESSING
⅓ cup tahini paste
3 Tbsp water
1 Tbsp lemon juice

1. Combine the red cabbage, cos lettuce and carrot in a bowl.

2. Whisk the dressing ingredients, pour over the salad and toss to combine.

3. Drape over the trout ribbons and sprinkle over the spring onions, coriander and sesame seeds.

4. Serve with lemon wedges on the side.

Prawn Skewer Salad

This unusual yet fun way to add prawns to a salad will take your guests by surprise. It certainly shows off the delicate pink prawns to perfection. There's also a touch of heat supplied by the chillies. If you're looking to create something a tad spicier, simply adjust the number of chillies used. This is a deceptively quick and easy salad to assemble that is as good to look at as it is to eat.

2 tsp olive oil
32 prawns, deveined and shelled, tails intact
salt and pepper to taste
1 Tbsp lemon juice
2–3 cups mixed salad leaves
½ cup torn fresh coriander
½ cup halved cherry tomatoes
2 fresh red chillies, sliced
3 spring onions, sliced
8 skewers
lemon wedges for serving

DRESSING
½ cup white wine
2 Tbsp red wine vinegar
¼ cup olive oil
1 Tbsp crushed garlic
salt and pepper to taste

1. Heat the olive oil in a frying pan, add the prawns, season with salt and pepper and pour over the lemon juice. Sauté until the prawns turn pink.

2. Arrange the remaining salad ingredients on a serving platter and season with salt and pepper.

3. Whisk the dressing ingredients and pour half over the salad.

4. Skewer 4 prawns per stick and place the skewers on top of the salad.

5. Pour over the remaining dressing and serve with lemon wedges.

Wicked Wasabi Tuna Salad

Many of us have had the experience of putting a tad too much wasabi on our sushi and suddenly being hit with some serious heat and that tickle up the nose. Luckily it fades quickly. Wasabi is a delicious addition to this dressing, as the tangy mayonnaise tempers the heat while still allowing that tell-tale burn to creep in. This robust salad is overflowing with good things, from the omega 3 in the tuna to the protein-rich lentils.

500g tuna steaks
2 Tbsp olive oil
ground black pepper to taste
2 cups mixed salad leaves
1 cup rocket
1 x 410g can lentils, drained and rinsed
2 spring onions, sliced
2 cups halved cherry tomatoes

MARINADE
¼ cup soy sauce
2 Tbsp sesame oil
2 Tbsp honey

2 Tbsp olive oil
½ tsp finely chopped fresh ginger
½ tsp finely chopped garlic

DRESSING
¼ cup tangy light mayonnaise
3 Tbsp wasabi paste
2 tsp chopped fresh thyme
4 tsp plain yoghurt
2 Tbsp olive oil
2 Tbsp water

1. Combine the marinade ingredients in a shallow, flat dish and add the tuna steaks. Marinate for about 30 minutes, turning the steaks halfway so that both sides are coated.

2. Heat the olive oil in a frying pan, liberally season the tuna steaks with ground black pepper and sear on both sides, being careful not to overcook the fish, as ideally it should be rare in the middle. Remove from the pan and allow to rest for about 5 minutes before slicing.

3. Arrange the salad leaves, rocket, lentils, spring onions and cherry tomatoes on a serving platter and top with the sliced tuna.

4. Whisk the dressing ingredients and pour over the salad.

Smoked Salmon and Citrus Salad

This unusual pairing of salty smoked salmon and sweet orange makes for a delectable flavour combination. The punchy rocket is the perfect foil for the citrusy dressing. Not to be outdone, there's the zing of the radish, the coolness of the cucumber and the creamy avocado, all brought together to create a salad packed full of sunshine flavours.

2 cups rocket
⅔ cup thinly sliced fennel bulb
10cm cucumber, diced
1 avocado, sliced
½ cup thinly sliced radish
200g smoked salmon ribbons
1 orange, segmented

DRESSING
¼ cup orange juice
2 Tbsp balsamic vinegar
1 Tbsp Dijon mustard
1 tsp honey
salt and pepper to taste

1. Place half the rocket on a platter and scatter over half the fennel, cucumber, avocado and radish.

2. Add the remaining rocket and top with the remaining fennel, cucumber, avocado and radish.

3. Drape the smoked salmon ribbons over the top and tuck the orange segments in between.

4. Whisk the dressing ingredients and pour over the salad.

Cajun Swordfish Salad

I enjoy eating swordfish. Its meaty texture and mild taste make it the ideal partner for Cajun seasoning. This bold rub is full of spicy, zesty flavours, which hark back to the kitchens of Louisiana, the home of Cajun cuisine. The coconut milk in the dressing is the perfect antidote to the kick from the rub, while the celery provides crunch and the cucumber coolness.

CAJUN RUB
2 tsp salt
2 tsp garlic powder
2 tsp paprika
1 tsp ground black pepper
½ tsp cayenne pepper
1 tsp dried origanum
1 tsp dried thyme

600g swordfish steak, filleted
1 Tbsp olive oil

1 large cucumber, sliced on the diagonal
2 stalks celery, chopped
1 cup roughly chopped baby spinach
½ cup roughly chopped fresh mint

DRESSING
¼ cup rice wine vinegar
½ cup coconut milk
salt and pepper to taste

1. Mix the ingredients for the Cajun rub.

2. Cut the swordfish into bite-size pieces and place into a sealable bag with the olive oil and Cajun rub. Gently massage the bag to ensure the fish is well coated. Place in the fridge for about 30 minutes to allow the flavours to develop.

3. Toss the cucumber, celery, baby spinach and mint in a serving bowl.

4. Heat a non-stick frying pan and sauté the swordfish for about 5 minutes until just cooked. Be careful not to overcook the fish, as it can become dry. Add a touch more olive oil if necessary. Allow to cool slightly before adding the fish to the salad.

5. Whisk the dressing ingredients and drizzle over the salad.

Chicken is truly the Swiss Army knife of proteins. It's light, lean, healthy and so versatile. Chicken salads are often drenched in mayonnaise and extra additives, and filled with unhealthy fats and calories, but it doesn't have to be this way. This assortment of succulent poultry salads is loaded with healthy fresh produce, contrasting textures and flavourful dressings.

This is poultry with pizzazz. These recipes use all parts of the bird and in a variety of ways, from chicken fillets and thighs to rotisserie style. I've also included some delectable duck and I invite you to swop these ingredients around for even more diversity.

It's not just about great taste and the feeling of lightness either, these recipes are also easy to follow and many can be prepared ahead. Enjoy a hassle-free midweek meal with the nutty apricot chicken salad, impress your guests with a decadent Asian duck salad or have fun with a chicken nacho salad over the weekend. No matter the occasion, you will find a salad to suit.

Poultry
Salads

Sassy Chicken Salsa Salad

Coriander goes by many names: in North America, they use the Spanish word cilantro, which refers to the leaves of the plant. In India, it's known as dhania and in China as Chinese parsley, which is not surprising, considering it's related to parsley and the leaves are quite similar. Whatever you call it, it's a great companion here to the chicken and salsa. A dash of chilli flakes gives a final kick to an already tasty dish.

4–5 skinless chicken breast fillets, cut into
    bite-size pieces
salt and pepper to taste
3 Tbsp olive oil
1 cup chopped celery
¼ cup chopped red onion
½ cup roughly chopped fresh coriander
¼ cup flaked almonds, roasted
2 Tbsp lime juice
½ tsp ground cumin

1 tsp garlic flakes
2 cups mixed salad leaves
dried chilli flakes for garnishing (optional)

SALSA
½ avocado, chopped
juice of 2 limes
½ cup chopped papaya
1 Tbsp chopped red onion
¼ cup chopped red pepper
salt and pepper to taste

1. Season the chicken with salt and pepper.

2. Heat 2 Tbsp olive oil in a frying pan and cook the chicken until golden on all sides and cooked through.

3. Transfer the chicken to a large bowl and add the celery, red onion, coriander and flaked almonds.

4. Mix the remaining olive oil with the lime juice, cumin and garlic flakes, pour over the chicken mixture and toss to combine.

5. Make the salsa in a separate bowl. Mix the avocado with the lime juice and add the papaya, red onion and red pepper. Stir gently and season with salt and pepper.

6. To assemble the salad, place the mixed salad leaves on a platter, add the chicken mixture and top with the salsa. Garnish with dried chilli flakes, if using.

Chicken Satay Salad

Who hasn't had a peanut butter craving? There's nothing more satisfying than sneaking a spoonful straight from the jar! So, when that craving strikes again, how about making it a little healthier and using it in a dressing for chicken instead? Adding some crunchy peanuts as a garnish helps heighten the nutritious nutty flavour. This is particularly delicious served with naan.

2 Tbsp olive oil
500g skinless deboned chicken thighs
3 cups store-bought coleslaw mix
1 cup sugar snap peas, sliced on the diagonal
1 cup cucumber rounds, quartered
3 Tbsp peanuts
3 Tbsp picked fresh coriander leaves

DRESSING
¼ cup crunchy peanut butter
½ cup coconut milk
¼ cup soy sauce

1. Heat the olive oil in a frying pan and sauté the chicken thighs until cooked and golden. Allow to rest for a couple of minutes before shredding the chicken.

2. Combine the coleslaw mix, sugar snap peas, cucumber and shredded chicken in a bowl. Dry roast the peanuts.

3. Mix the dressing ingredients and pour over the salad. Toss until well combined and garnish with the coriander leaves and roasted peanuts.

Nutty Apricot Chicken Salad

Use juicy dried apricots that are still quite soft to the touch. These sweet apricots sit comfortably in the citrus dressing, as if they were made for each other. In fact, the dressing is the real star here and is full of flavour with the aromatic cumin, the bite of the apple cider vinegar and the sweetness of the honey. Roasting the almonds gives them a more complex and nutty flavour and a crisper texture, which gives the salad the crunchiness it needs.

4–6 skinless chicken breast fillets,
   halved lengthways
salt and pepper to taste
1 Tbsp olive oil
2–3 cups mixed salad leaves
50g dried apricots, halved
¼ cup flaked almonds, roasted

DRESSING
½ cup olive oil
1 Tbsp fresh orange juice
1 Tbsp apple cider vinegar
1 tsp honey
1 tsp paprika
1 tsp ground cumin
1 Tbsp chopped fresh flat-leaf parsley
½ tsp finely chopped garlic
salt and pepper to taste

1. Season the chicken fillets with salt and pepper.

2. Heat the olive oil in a large frying pan over medium heat and sauté the chicken until cooked. Slice into bite-size pieces and set aside.

3. Whizz the dressing ingredients using a hand blender until well combined.

4. Place all the ingredients in a bowl and toss well.

5. Pour over the dressing and toss gently to coat.

Chimichurri Chicken Salad

Chimichurri has been popping up on menus recently and is remarkably easy to put together. This parsley-based sauce originated in Argentina and Uruguay and is traditionally used on grilled meats. It's the consummate companion to this healthy salad, though, providing the spice to the cos's crunch and the avocados' creaminess.

4–6 skinless chicken breast fillets, halved lengthways
2 Tbsp olive oil
2–3 cups roughly torn cos lettuce
3–4 tomatoes, sliced
½ red onion, finely sliced
2 avocados, sliced

DRESSING
¾ cup olive oil
2½ Tbsp red wine vinegar
2 Tbsp chopped fresh parsley
4 cloves garlic, finely chopped
3–4 Tbsp chopped fresh chilli
½ tsp dried origanum

1. Whizz the dressing ingredients using a hand blender to form a smooth sauce. Rest in the fridge for at least 10 minutes to allow the flavours to develop. You can even prepare it the day before and keep it in the fridge until ready to use.

2. Pour ¼ cup of the dressing into a shallow dish, add the chicken fillets and marinate for about 20 minutes, turning halfway to ensure both sides are coated.

3. Heat the olive oil in a frying pan and fry the chicken fillets until golden and cooked through. Slice into strips.

4. Place the salad ingredients onto a platter, top with the chicken strips and drizzle over the remaining dressing.

Crunchy Smoked Chicken Salad

This is a super-easy salad to rustle up. The beauty of smoked chicken is that, because it has been smoked, it has a long fridge life. It has therefore become a staple in my home. Another ingredient I always have on hand are croutons. I keep them in the freezer and whip them out when needed. They thaw quickly, and if you find they're a little soggy, a few minutes in the oven is all that's needed to bring back their crunchiness.

2 smoked chicken breasts, sliced
1½ cups rocket
1½ cups roughly torn fresh coriander
½ cup croutons
salt to taste

DRESSING
2 tsp wholegrain mustard
2 Tbsp plain yoghurt
¼ cup olive oil
1 tsp sherry vinegar
1 tsp honey
1 Tbsp water
salt and pepper to taste

1. Toss the chicken, rocket, coriander and croutons in a bowl and season with salt.

2. Whisk the dressing ingredients and drizzle over the salad.

Chicken Frittata Salad

A rotisserie chicken is ideal for this salad, as it cuts down on prep. Simply shred the chicken from the bone, and voila! The meat is moist and ready to use. The mushrooms and frittata make an unusual base, but provide some additional wow and flavour. Although this takes some time to make, it's certainly worth the effort.

4 tsp olive oil
2 cups sliced button mushrooms
2 Tbsp sherry vinegar
1 tsp dried rosemary
⅔ cup halved or quartered cherry tomatoes
½ cup canned chickpeas, drained and rinsed
2–3 cups shredded rotisserie chicken
1 tsp dried thyme
8 eggs
4 tsp chutney
salt and pepper to taste
4 tsp butter
½ cup grated Cheddar cheese
2 cups roughly torn rocket
1 cup chopped cucumber

DRESSING
4 tsp chutney
4 tsp olive oil
4 tsp water
salt and pepper to taste

1. Heat the olive oil in a large frying pan and sauté the mushrooms until just softened.

2. Add the sherry vinegar and rosemary and continue to sauté until the mushrooms start to brown.

3. Stir in the cherry tomatoes, chickpeas, chicken and thyme and continue to sauté until heated through. Remove from the heat and set aside.

4. Whisk the eggs and chutney in a bowl until well combined. Season with salt and pepper.

5. Melt 1 tsp butter in a crêpe pan, pour in a quarter of the egg mixture and cook like a frittata until just done. Transfer to a serving plate and repeat until all the frittatas are cooked.

6. Top each frittata with some grated Cheddar, followed by the rocket, chicken mixture and cucumber.

7. Whisk the dressing ingredients and drizzle some over each frittata.

Curried Chicken
with Pistachios and Raisins

This salad is overflowing with healthy ingredients. Although pistachios are regarded as nuts, botanically speaking they're actually seeds. They originated in western Asia and archaeologists have found evidence that they were eaten as far back as 7 000 BC. Raisins, although also small in size, pack a nutritional punch. When grapes are dehydrated, the nutrients become more concentrated, and raisins are thus full of vitamin B, iron and potassium. The sweetness of the raisins balances beautifully here with the curried chicken, while the pistachios provide the crunch.

2 tsp curry powder
2 tsp garlic flakes
2 tsp onion powder
salt and pepper to taste
4–6 skinless chicken breast fillets,
   halved lengthways
2 Tbsp olive oil
180ml Greek yoghurt
2 Tbsp honey

¼ cup raisins
⅓ cup pistachios, shelled and roughly chopped
3 cups mixed salad leaves
1 cup grated carrot
¼ cup roughly chopped fresh parsley

DRESSING
¼ cup olive oil
1 tsp white wine vinegar
salt and pepper to taste

1. Combine the curry powder, garlic flakes, onion powder, salt and pepper in a small bowl and season the chicken fillets with half of it.

2. Heat the olive oil in a frying pan and sauté the chicken until cooked. Slice into bite-size pieces and mix with the remaining curry rub until well coated.

3. Combine the yoghurt, honey, raisins and pistachios in a large bowl, keeping some of the raisins and pistachios aside for garnishing. Add the chicken and mix well.

4. Whisk the dressing ingredients until well combined.

5. To assemble, place the salad leaves, carrot and parsley on a platter, pour over the dressing and toss to coat. Place the chicken on top and scatter over the remaining raisins and pistachios.

Herbed Cranberry and Chicken Salad

The secret to keeping this salad looking attractive is to dress it halfway so that the fragrant herbs retain their vibrant greens and don't arrive at the table limp and soggy. Herbs are such a useful way to add flavour and texture to a salad. The slightly spicy chives contrast perfectly with the sweet cranberries, while the earthy parsley balances beautifully next to the stimulating blue cheese. All in all, these herbs provide an unexpected punch of flavour to this salad.

400–600g skinless deboned chicken thighs
1 tsp dried thyme
salt and pepper to taste
1 tsp olive oil
¼ cup water, or as needed
2 cups mixed salad leaves
½ red onion, thinly sliced
½ cup sliced chives
½ cup torn fresh parsley
½ cup torn fresh dill
¼ cup crumbled blue cheese

DRESSING
2 Tbsp red wine vinegar
¼ cup olive oil
¾ cup dried cranberries, plus extra for garnishing
1 Tbsp Dijon mustard
1 clove garlic, finely chopped
3–4 Tbsp water
salt and pepper to taste

1. Season the chicken thighs with the thyme, salt and pepper.

2. Heat the olive oil in a frying pan and brown the chicken thighs on all sides. Cook the chicken until done, adding the water if the pan gets dry. Remove from the heat and allow to cool before slicing the chicken.

3. Using a hand blender, whizz the dressing ingredients until smooth.

4. Combine the mixed salad leaves with half the chicken and the red onion in a serving bowl. Season with salt and pepper and pour over half the dressing. Toss to combine.

5. Scatter over the chives, parsley, dill and blue cheese.

6. Add the remaining chicken, drizzle over the rest of the dressing and garnish with extra dried cranberries.

Smoky Chicken Pasta Salad

Smoked paprika is the ideal counterbalance to what can sometimes be quite a bland meat, so banish the bland with this smoky, somewhat spicy rub. Grilling the aubergine and peppers adds another layer of smokiness, while the crumbly feta supplies the saltiness and the delicate avocado the creaminess. This salad is also brimming with healthy capsicum, both from the peppers and the cayenne pepper. As if you needed any more reason to tuck into this satisfying salad.

1 medium aubergine
1 green pepper
2 red peppers
¼ cup olive oil
150–200g penne pasta
4–5 skinless chicken breast fillets,
   halved lengthways
2 baby marrows, sliced into ribbons
2 rounds feta, crumbled
1 avocado, chopped
microgreens for garnishing

RUB
1 Tbsp smoked paprika
1 Tbsp salt
1 Tbsp brown sugar
¼–½ tsp chilli powder
½ tsp ground black pepper
½ tsp garlic powder
½ tsp onion powder
¼ tsp ground cumin
¼ tsp cayenne pepper

DRESSING
¼ cup orange juice
¼ cup olive oil
2 Tbsp honey
salt and pepper to taste

1. Preheat the oven to 200°C.

2. Place the aubergine and peppers on a greased baking sheet and drizzle each with 1 tsp olive oil. Bake for about 20 minutes until the vegetables start to char, then turn on the grill for about 5 minutes.

3. Remove from the oven and allow to cool before removing the skins from the aubergine and peppers. Cut the vegetables into chunks.

4. Cook the pasta according to the packet instructions. Drain and set aside to cool.

5. Combine the rub ingredients in a shallow, flat dish and coat the chicken fillets.

6. Add the remaining olive oil to a frying pan and cook the chicken until browned and cooked through. Allow to cool before slicing.

7. Place the cooled pasta and roasted vegetables in a bowl along with the baby marrows, feta and avocado. Stir carefully to mix, then add the chicken.

8. Whisk the dressing ingredients and drizzle over the salad. Toss carefully to coat and garnish with microgreens.

Chicken Nacho Salad

Chips in a salad, you ask? Why not? Although not strictly crisps, tortilla chips certainly satisfy the same craving for me. Putting them in a salad makes me feel less guilty about tucking into them, too. This salad has many of the ingredients you associate with a gooey, calorie-laden plate of nachos, but without the fat. Sure, it has some sour cream, but it also has heaps of healthiness from the juicy tomatoes to the protein-packed spinach. So go on, tuck in.

2 tsp ground cumin
2 tsp smoked paprika
½–1 tsp chilli powder
½ Tbsp salt
4–6 skinless chicken breast fillets,
  halved lengthways
2 Tbsp olive oil
¼ cup chicken stock
2 Tbsp lime juice
2–3 large tomatoes, chopped
1 large avocado, chopped
1 cup loosely packed coriander, plus extra
  for garnishing
1½ cups loosely packed baby spinach
115g tortilla chips, plus extra for garnishing
¼ cup sour cream

DRESSING
¼ cup olive oil
zest of 1 lime
2 Tbsp lime juice
1 clove garlic, finely chopped
½ tsp dried origanum
1 tsp grated fresh ginger
½ tsp ground cumin
salt and pepper to taste

1. Mix the cumin, paprika, chilli powder and salt in a flat, shallow dish. Coat the chicken fillets in this spice mixture.

2. Heat the olive oil in a frying pan over medium heat and cook the chicken until almost done. Remove the chicken from the pan and set aside to rest for about 5 minutes before cutting into chunks.

3. Add the chicken stock and lime juice to the same pan and stir to combine. Return the chicken to the pan and simmer for a few minutes until fully cooked.

4. Whisk the dressing ingredients until well combined.

5. Place the tomatoes and avocado in a bowl, pour over the dressing and toss gently to coat.

6. Roughly chop the coriander and baby spinach.

7. Layer a third of the tortilla chips in a serving dish. Scatter over a third of the chicken mixture and dollop with some sour cream. Add a third of the avocado and tomato mixture and sprinkle over a third of the coriander and baby spinach.

8. Repeat the layers, garnishing the top with some crushed tortilla chips and coriander sprigs.

Colourful Chicken and Beetroot Salad

I love the way the briny feta in this salad takes on a pretty pink hue thanks to the beetroot. The couscous adds some real substance, making this perfect for a main course to serve day or night. Couscous is often mistaken for a grain, but it's actually a type of pasta, made with semolina flour from durum wheat. No matter what name you give it, it's really quick and easy to prepare. The cool and sweet mint rounds off this enjoyable and vibrant salad.

2 medium beetroots
1 cup cooked couscous
400–600g rotisserie chicken, shredded
2 spring onions, sliced
1 cup baby spinach
1½ rounds feta, cubed
¾ cup halved cherry tomatoes
3 Tbsp roughly chopped fresh mint
1 Tbsp pine nuts, roasted

DRESSING
⅓ cup olive oil
zest and juice of 2 medium lemons
1 clove garlic, finely chopped
salt and pepper to taste

1. Boil the beetroots in a saucepan of water until soft, then drain and set aside to cool. Once cooled, peel and quarter the beetroots.

2. Place the beetroots, couscous, chicken, spring onions, baby spinach, feta and cherry tomatoes in a bowl and toss to combine.

3. Whisk the dressing ingredients and pour over the salad, tossing well. Finally, scatter over the mint and roasted pine nuts.

Asian Duck Salad

This elegant salad is perfect to serve at a luncheon. The dressing has all the ingredients we associate with Asia, namely hoisin sauce, fish sauce and soy sauce, which when combined with the other ingredients, create a wonderful umami flavour. The peppery watercress and fresh cucumber are the perfect antidote to the rich, meaty duck. This luxury salad, full of bold Asian flavours, is sure to wow your guests.

4–6 duck breasts
2 tsp five-spice powder
1 clove garlic, finely sliced
2 spring onions, finely chopped
2 tsp sesame oil
2–3 cups watercress
1 fresh red chilli, deseeded and julienned
½ cup diagonally sliced mange tout
2 spring onions, sliced
½ cucumber, cut into ribbons
¼ cup finely sliced radish
bean sprouts for garnishing

fresh parsley for garnishing
microgreens for garnishing
toasted white sesame seeds for garnishing

DRESSING
2 Tbsp soy sauce
1 tsp grated fresh ginger
¼ cup hoisin sauce
¼ cup olive oil
2 Tbsp fish sauce
salt and pepper to taste

1. Score the skin of the duck breasts with a criss-cross pattern making sure not to cut all the way to the flesh. Season with the five-spice powder, garlic and spring onions.

2. Place the sesame oil in a frying pan, add the duck breasts skin-side down and slowly heat the pan. This will melt the fat and help the skin to crisp up without burning.

3. Fry for 10–15 minutes until the skin is crisp and brown and as much of the visible white fat as possible has melted away. Remove from the heat and rest the duck breasts for 10 minutes before slicing across the grain.

4. Place the watercress, chilli, mange tout, spring onions, cucumber and radish on a platter and toss to combine. Place the sliced duck on top.

5. Whisk the dressing ingredients and pour over the salad, then garnish with bean sprouts, fresh parsley, microgreens and toasted sesame seeds.

Shaved Asparagus, Peppadew and Chicken Salad

There's no need to cook shaved asparagus because it's thin enough to eat as is. Asparagus has been used for centuries and has even been found in some ancient Egyptian tombs. The word comes from Greek, meaning 'to spring up', no doubt because asparagus plants grow straight up, like spears. They're not only ancient, they're also healthy, full of vitamins and high doses of folic acid.

4–5 skinless chicken breast fillets, cut into strips
½ tsp dried mixed herbs
salt and pepper to taste
3 Tbsp olive oil
2–3 cups baby spinach
2 spring onions, sliced on the diagonal
150g fresh asparagus spears, shaved
7–10 mild peppadews, roughly chopped
1–2 large mozzarella balls, torn into bite-size pieces
juice of ½ lemon
2 Tbsp white sesame seeds, toasted

DRESSING
½ cup Greek yoghurt
2 tsp wholegrain mustard
½ tsp crushed garlic
salt and pepper to taste

1. Season the chicken strips with the dried mixed herbs, salt and pepper.

2. Heat 1 Tbsp olive oil in a frying pan and fry the chicken strips until golden and just cooked. Be careful not to overcook them.

3. Scatter the baby spinach over a platter and add the spring onions, asparagus shavings, peppadews and mozzarella.

4. Place the chicken strips on top and drizzle over the remaining olive oil and the lemon juice.

5. Combine the dressing ingredients and pour over the salad. Garnish with the toasted sesame seeds.

Thai Coconut Chicken Salad

Poaching chicken in coconut milk is the ideal way to create creamy, tender chicken. The low temperature and moisture stop the chicken from cooking too quickly and drying out. The addition of paprika adds a dose of colour to the chicken, which could otherwise look a tad bland. Extra zing is added with as much green curry paste as you can handle. The aromatic fresh herbs and crunchy mange tout are other important role players in this Thai-inspired feast.

1 x 400g can coconut milk
5 Tbsp lime juice
2 tsp fish sauce
1½–2 Tbsp green curry paste
1 bay leaf
salt to taste
4–5 skinless chicken breast fillets,
   halved lengthways
paprika for seasoning

2–3 cups baby spinach
15cm cucumber, diced
135g mange tout, sliced
¼ cup thinly sliced chives
3 Tbsp torn fresh coriander leaves
3 Tbsp torn fresh mint leaves
3 Tbsp torn fresh basil leaves
3 Tbsp olive oil
2 Tbsp desiccated coconut, toasted

1. Place the coconut milk, 2 Tbsp lime juice, fish sauce, curry paste and bay leaf in a saucepan. Season with salt and bring to a gentle simmer over low–medium heat.

2. Add the chicken, season with paprika and poach gently, with the lid on, for about 15 minutes until the chicken is tender.

3. Remove and shred the chicken, then return it to the saucepan, stirring to coat completely.

4. Place the baby spinach, cucumber, mange tout, chives, coriander, mint and basil in a bowl and toss gently to combine.

5. Drizzle over the olive oil and remaining lime juice and toss to coat the leaves.

6. Add the chicken in its sauce and sprinkle over the toasted coconut.

Olé Chicken Salad

Here we have all the features of a taco, except for the shell. And when I think tacos, I think Mexico. And when I think Mexico, I think tequila. But instead of margaritas, let's make a salad. The fiery spirit adds a tempting kick to chicken. Here it's no holds barred, as the tequila is in the marinade and the dressing. Definitely for adults only.

4–5 skinless chicken breast fillets, cut into strips
1 Tbsp olive oil
2 cups mixed salad leaves
1 cup shredded red cabbage
1 tomato, diced
½ red onion, finely chopped
½ cup drained whole kernel corn
½ cup julienned carrot
¼ cup sliced jalapeño chilli
1 avocado, sliced
salt and pepper to taste
lime wedges for serving

MARINADE

3 Tbsp olive oil
3 Tbsp tequila
1 Tbsp lime juice
1 tsp crushed garlic
½ tsp ground coriander
½ tsp dried origanum
1 tsp honey
salt and pepper to taste

DRESSING

¼ cup olive oil
2 Tbsp tequila
1 Tbsp lime juice
½ tsp honey
1 Tbsp roughly chopped fresh coriander

1. Combine the marinade ingredients.

2. Place the chicken strips in a sealable bag, add the marinade and massage the bag to coat the chicken. Refrigerate for at least 1 hour to marinate.

3. Heat the olive oil in a frying pan and add the chicken along with any residual marinade. Fry until the chicken is golden and just cooked. Be careful not to overcook it.

4. Whizz the dressing ingredients using a hand blender and set aside.

5. Combine the mixed salad leaves, red cabbage, tomato, onion, corn kernels, carrot and chilli in a bowl and then transfer to a platter.

6. Place the avocado and chicken strips on top and season with salt and pepper.

7. Pour over the dressing and serve with lime wedges.

For some, a meal isn't complete without something meaty, but that's no reason to ditch salads. This mouth watering selection of meaty salads offers a range that will satisfy the protein craving while getting those all important greens in at the same time.

Jazz up your dinners by combining your favourite ingredients in fresh ways to create wholesome and satisfying meals that hit the spot. Healthy ostrich, good old biltong and venison are some of the more exotic additions, but the succulence of a good rump or fillet and the spicy flavour of chorizo all make an appearance.

If you're watching your calorie intake, this salad selection is an amazing way to include protein in your diet without adding extra calories. Packed with extra protein, these salads are a tasty option for those of you who want to build muscle or get your strength up.

Whether you hanker for a green pea and lamb salad or prefer a beef tagliata, this collection has something for every meat lover. You'll be sure to find a new favourite with this beefy, brawny and bold flavoured salad assortment.

.

Meat
Salads

Peachy Parma Ham Salad

This easy and refreshing salad works equally well as a starter. Think Parma ham and melon, but with a twist. Instead of melon, how about some grilled peaches? Grilling gives the peaches an intense, caramelised taste, which is splendidly offset by the salty, moist Parma ham. Afficionados all agree that the fat is an important part of the meat, creating a satisfying, complex flavour, so don't be tempted to cut it off.

2 peaches, cut into wedges
2 tsp olive oil
2 cups loosely packed watercress
2 cups loosely packed rocket
200g Parma ham, sliced
½ cup roughly chopped walnuts
100g goat's cheese, torn

DRESSING
2 Tbsp orange juice
2 Tbsp olive oil
2 tsp honey
½ tsp apple cider vinegar
salt and pepper to taste

1. Heat a griddle pan until hot. Toss the peach wedges in the olive oil and cook on all sides until griddle lines appear.

2. Place the watercress, rocket and peaches on a platter and drape over the Parma ham.

3. Scatter over the walnuts and goat's cheese.

4. Whisk the dressing ingredients and pour over the salad.

Sesame-coated Beef and Asparagus Salad

Miso is central to traditional Japanese cuisine. Made from fermented soybeans, it comes in two varieties: white and red. White miso has a shorter maturing period than red, hence the colour difference, and is also sweeter and milder, making it ideal for salad dressings. Drizzled over perfectly seared beef, charred asparagus and golden mushrooms, this Asian-inspired dressing is fit for an emperor.

400–500g beef fillet
salt and pepper to taste
3 Tbsp olive oil
5 large brown mushrooms, sliced
100–150g fresh baby asparagus spears
¼ cup white sesame seeds, toasted
3–4 cups mixed salad leaves

DRESSING
1 Tbsp olive oil
1 Tbsp rice wine vinegar
1 Tbsp soy sauce
2 tsp white miso paste
2 tsp honey
salt and pepper to taste

1. Season the beef fillet generously with salt and pepper.

2. Heat 2 Tbsp olive oil in a frying pan until hot and sear the fillet on all sides. Cook to preference and remove from the pan. Allow to rest for about 10 minutes before slicing.

3. Wipe the pan, add the remaining olive oil and sauté the mushrooms until tender and golden. Remove the mushrooms and set aside.

4. Sauté the asparagus spears in the same pan until tender and charred.

5. Place the toasted sesame seeds on a plate and coat the beef slices.

6. Arrange the mixed salad leaves on a platter and top with the mushrooms, asparagus spears and the sesame-coated beef.

7. Whisk the dressing ingredients and drizzle over the salad.

Spiced Salami Salad

Salami is most often associated with sandwiches or charcuterie platters, but it's also a delicious meat option for a salad. Due to its strong flavour, it stands up well to squeaky halloumi. Although not everyone agrees that salami should be cooked, I like the effect of heat on this cured meat. It makes it slightly harder and separates the fat, which I simply dab off. What everyone does agree on is that halloumi, when grilled, reveals a strong, savoury and almost smoky flavour with a mouth-watering, creamy texture.

1 tsp olive oil
250g broccolini
150–200g salami, sliced
250g halloumi, cut into 1cm-thick slices
½ cup roughly chopped fresh parsley

DRESSING
2 tsp oil from cooking the salami
1 clove garlic, crushed
1 tsp lemon zest
2 Tbsp tomato paste
¼ cup pomegranate or cranberry juice
1 tsp Dijon mustard
1 tsp balsamic vinegar

1. Heat the olive oil in a frying pan and sauté the broccolini until they start to char. Remove from the pan and set aside.

2. In the same pan, sauté the salami slices until they just start to crisp. You might need to do this in batches. Remove the salami from the pan and drain on paper towel before cutting the slices in half.

3. Whisk the dressing ingredients and set aside.

4. In the pan you used to cook the salami, grill the halloumi slices on both sides until golden.

5. Place the broccolini on a platter, top with the salami and halloumi, pour over the dressing and scatter over the chopped fresh parsley.

Beef Tagliata

Tagliata means 'to cut' in Italian, which aptly describes this popular Italian dish made with thinly sliced pieces of meat. Conventionally, it's served with rocket and shaved Parmesan, but I've upped the ante somewhat by adding mushrooms cooked in sherry vinegar and a few drops of white truffle oil. White truffles are a true Italian delicacy; with their pungent aroma and subtle flavour, they turn any ordinary dish into a gourmet taste sensation.

2 Tbsp olive oil
2 cups portobellini mushrooms
1 clove garlic, crushed
1 Tbsp sherry vinegar
2 tsp chopped fresh thyme
600–700g beef fillet
salt and pepper to taste
2 cups small mixed tomatoes
3–4 cups rocket
1 cup shaved Parmesan

DRESSING

2 tsp tangy light mayonnaise
2 Tbsp plain yoghurt
4 tsp water
1 tsp white truffle oil
salt and pepper to taste

1. Heat half the olive oil in a frying pan until quite hot. Add the mushrooms and coat well in the oil, but then do not stir again until the mushrooms have released all their liquid and turned golden.

2. Reduce the heat, add the garlic and sherry vinegar and continue to cook until the vinegar has evaporated. Remove from the heat and scatter over the fresh thyme.

3. Season the beef fillet generously with salt and pepper.

4. Heat the remaining olive oil in another large frying pan until hot. Sear the fillet on all sides, then reduce the heat and continue to cook until done to your liking. I prefer my fillet rare. Remove the fillet from the pan and allow to rest for 5–10 minutes before slicing thinly.

5. In the same pan, sauté the tomatoes until they start to char. Be careful not to overcook them.

6. Place the rocket on a platter, scatter over the mushrooms and tomatoes, and drape over the fillet slices. Scatter over the Parmesan.

7. Whisk the dressing ingredients and pour over the salad.

Venison Carpaccio Salad

This sublime salad is a kaleidoscope of colours and textures, and although it may seem like a lot of ingredients, they each have their part to play. I find it easier to buy carpaccio already sliced, and venison is always a good choice, as the meat has very little fat. The sweetness from the mandarin orange and mango counteracts the somewhat gamey taste of the meat, creating a perfect harmony of flavours, while the seeds add a final layer of texture.

1 cup mixed salad leaves
10 button mushrooms, quartered
150g canned mandarin orange segments (reserve
   syrup for dressing)
1 mango, chopped
300–400g venison carpaccio
1 avocado, thinly sliced
2 Tbsp slivered almonds
1 Tbsp sunflower seeds
1 Tbsp white sesame seeds, toasted
1 Tbsp black sesame seeds
pea shoots for garnishing

DRESSING
½ cup olive oil
½ tsp crushed garlic
2 Tbsp finely chopped spring onion
2 Tbsp brown sugar
1 tsp soy sauce
1 Tbsp balsamic vinegar
1 tsp curry powder
1 tsp salt
2 Tbsp mandarin orange syrup

1. Whizz the dressing ingredients using a hand blender until well combined. Refrigerate until ready to use.

2. Place the mixed salad leaves and butter lettuce on a platter and scatter over the cherry tomatoes, mushrooms, mandarin orange segments and mango.

3. Drape the carpaccio slices over the salad and top with the avocado.

4. Scatter over the slivered almonds and all the seeds, garnish with pea shoots and drizzle over the dressing.

Wood-smoked Bacon Salad

There is an array of flavours and textures at play here, from the deliciously creamy avocado to the subtly sweet dressing and crunchy walnuts, all working in unison with the woody bacon and tart goat's cheese. Nestled on a bed of rocket, this is a quick and easy salad to whip up, making it a great option for Sunday dinners or when you don't feel like eating anything too filling.

250g wood-smoked back bacon
150g goat's cheese, sliced into 1cm-thick rounds
4 cups rocket
2 avocados, sliced
½ cup roughly broken walnuts

DRESSING
1 Tbsp water
1 Tbsp lemon juice
2 Tbsp tangy light mayonnaise
2 Tbsp full-cream plain yoghurt
salt and pepper to taste

1. Fry the bacon in a pan over medium heat until crispy. When cool enough to handle, break into pieces and set aside.

2. Heat the oven's grill. Place the goat's cheese slices on a greased baking sheet and grill for a few minutes until the cheese starts to turn golden. Don't leave it in for too long or it will become too soft.

3. Place the rocket on a platter, scatter over the bacon bits, add the sliced avocados and place the melted goat's cheese around the edges.

4. Whisk the dressing ingredients and pour over the salad. Finally, scatter over the walnuts and serve immediately.

Biltong Salad

This is an easy, no-cook salad that's sure to impress your foreign friends. As South Africans, we're used to snacking on biltong, but it works equally well as the star ingredient in this salad. The dressing is the co-star, full of complexity and flavour, with the paprika adding a smoky element to the slightly sweet yet tangy mustard. Finished off with some crunchy cashews, you have a delightful dish brimming with protein.

1 red onion, finely chopped
¼ cup roughly chopped capers
2 cloves garlic, finely chopped
½ cup roughly chopped fresh parsley
2–3 cups cos lettuce
300g biltong, thinly sliced
¼ cup grated Parmesan
½ cup cashew nuts, roasted

DRESSING
2 Tbsp red wine vinegar
6 Tbsp olive oil
1 Tbsp lime juice
½ tsp smoked paprika
1 clove garlic, crushed
½ tsp dried origanum
1 Tbsp honey mustard
salt and pepper to taste

1. Whizz the dressing ingredients using a hand blender and set aside.

2. In a separate bowl, combine the red onion, capers, garlic, parsley and half the dressing. Toss to combine.

3. Arrange half the lettuce on a platter, scatter over half the biltong and add half the onion mixture. Repeat the layers, then drizzle over the remaining dressing and scatter over the Parmesan and cashew nuts.

Green Pea and Lamb Salad

Peas aren't normally recognised as a salad ingredient, but I believe they're undervalued. You can always rely on them to provide a glorious bolt of colour to your plate. Botanically speaking they're actually a fruit, because they contain seeds. They also provide a surprising amount of nutrients, are high in fibre and protein, and have a low glycaemic index. Peas always taste extra good with mint, and lamb and mint are great companions, so combining all three is sure to be a winner.

500–600g lamb chump chops, deboned and
   fat removed
1 cup frozen peas
2 baby marrows, sliced into thin rounds
2 rounds feta, crumbled
16 olives, pitted and halved
2 Tbsp roughly chopped fresh dill
2 Tbsp roughly chopped fresh parsley
2 Tbsp roughly chopped fresh mint
2 spring onions, thinly sliced

MARINADE
2 Tbsp olive oil
1 tsp chopped fresh thyme
4 tsp lemon juice
1 clove garlic, finely chopped

DRESSING
¼ cup olive oil
2 tsp lemon zest
3 Tbsp lemon juice
1 clove garlic, finely chopped
salt and pepper to taste

1. Mix the marinade ingredients in a bowl.

2. Cut the lamb into cubes and add to the marinade, stirring to ensure the lamb is well coated. Leave to marinate for 30–60 minutes.

3. Blanch the frozen peas in boiling water for 1–2 minutes, then remove and refresh in cold water.

4. Heat a frying pan over medium–high heat and sauté the lamb cubes until just cooked.

5. Combine the peas with the rest of the salad ingredients in a serving bowl and add the lamb.

6. Whisk the dressing ingredients, pour over the salad and toss well to combine.

Vietnamese Pork Salad

Fish sauce is an essential ingredient in Asian cuisine and I've used it here in both the marinade and the dressing. It has a rather pungent aroma, but acts more like a salt, creating a savoury umami taste explosion. Another Asian staple is sesame oil, which has a distinctive nutty taste and aroma. Sesame has been around for centuries and was one of the first crops used for oil production.

500–600g pork loin, cut into 1cm cubes
2 tsp sesame oil
1½ cups finely sliced white cabbage
1 yellow pepper, julienned
½ cup loosely packed fresh basil
½ cup loosely packed rocket
½ cup loosely packed baby spinach
10–12 sugar snap peas, sliced on the diagonal
bean sprouts for garnishing
dried chilli flakes for garnishing (optional)

MARINADE
1 Tbsp grated fresh ginger
2 cloves garlic, crushed
2 tsp fish sauce
2 Tbsp soy sauce
1 Tbsp honey
2 tsp sesame oil

DRESSING
2 Tbsp rice wine vinegar
2 Tbsp lemon juice
½ cup olive oil
1 Tbsp honey
2 tsp fish sauce

1. Whisk the marinade ingredients and pour into a sealable bag. Add the pork and massage the bag to ensure the cubes are well coated. Leave in the fridge to marinate for about an hour.

2. Heat the sesame oil in a frying pan until hot. Sear the pork cubes on all sides, then lower the heat and continue to cook until done. Allow to rest for a few minutes.

3. Toss the pork with the salad ingredients in a serving bowl.

4. Whisk the dressing ingredients, pour over the salad and toss well.

5. Garnish with bean sprouts and chilli flakes, if using.

Spicy Sirloin Salad

In North America, cos lettuce is called romaine. While Cos is the Greek island on which this lettuce originated, it reached Europe via Rome, where its Italian name is lattuga romana, which simply means 'Roman lettuce', hence romaine. Whatever you call it, it still has that characteristic crunch. Here it works in perfect unison with the spicy sirloin.

500–600g sirloin steak, fat removed
1 Tbsp canola oil
1–2 cups torn rocket
1½ cups torn cos lettuce
1 cup halved cherry tomatoes
2 avocados, sliced
1½ cups croutons
100g goat's cheese, torn

RUB
2 tsp paprika
1 tsp garlic flakes
½ tsp chilli powder
salt to taste

DRESSING
6 Tbsp olive oil
4 tsp red wine vinegar
½ tsp Dijon mustard
½ tsp honey
salt and pepper to taste

1. Mix the rub ingredients, seasoning generously with salt. Rub all over the sirloin steak, ensuring it is well coated.

2. Heat the canola oil in a frying pan until hot and sear the steak on all sides. Cook to preference – I like mine medium rare. Allow the steak to rest for about 10 minutes before slicing.

3. Whisk the dressing ingredients and set aside

4. Arrange the rocket, cos lettuce, cherry tomatoes and avocados on a platter.

5. Place the steak slices on top, scatter over the croutons and goat's cheese and drizzle over the dressing.

Sunday Salad with Roast Beef and Potato

There's nothing quite like a Sunday lunch resplendent with roast beef, potatoes, greens and the requisite horseradish. This salad has all the right elements and can be eaten cold or at room temperature. Instead of gravy, I've made a horseradish dressing. I use light mayonnaise, as it has all the tanginess of normal mayonnaise without the extra calories.

200–300g baby potatoes
2–3 cups loosely packed baby spinach
500–600g roast beef, sliced
2 Tbsp chopped chives

DRESSING
¼ cup creamed horseradish
2 Tbsp lemon juice
2 Tbsp water
¼ cup tangy light mayonnaise

1. Cook the baby potatoes in their skins in a saucepan of salted boiling water until tender. Drain and allow to cool before halving if too big.

2. Whisk the dressing ingredients and pour over the potatoes, tossing to coat evenly.

3. Arrange the baby spinach on a platter, add the potatoes, place the roast beef slices on top and scatter over the chopped chives.

Blue Cheese Steak Salad

Minute steak is often confused with cube steak, but they're actually from two different cuts. Minute steak is thinly sliced sirloin, whereas cube steak comes from the tougher cuts and needs a machine, much like a mallet, to soften it, which gives cube steak its signature indentations. Minute steak, because it's cut so thinly, doesn't require tenderising. It's also really quick and easy to cook, so it's ideal to use for salads.

4 tsp olive oil
500g minute steak
3 cups mixed salad leaves
1 cup sliced radish
½ medium red onion, sliced
2 nectarines or plums, cut into chunks
½ cup crumbled blue cheese

RUB
1 Tbsp smoked paprika
1 tsp dried origanum
1 tsp ground coriander
1 tsp ground black pepper
2 tsp salt
½ tsp garlic powder
½ tsp onion powder

DRESSING
6 Tbsp olive oil
2 Tbsp chutney
4 tsp white wine vinegar
salt and pepper to taste

1. Mix the rub ingredients. Drizzle 2 tsp olive oil over the minute steaks and coat them in the rub.

2. Heat the remaining olive oil in a frying pan and grill the steaks until just done. Allow the steaks to rest for a few minutes before slicing.

3. Toss the lettuce, radish and red onion in a bowl, add the steak slices and nectarines or plums, and sprinkle over the blue cheese.

4. Whisk the dressing ingredients and pour over the salad.

Crunchy Chorizo Salad

You can whip up this salad in no time at all. Chorizo is known for its somewhat spicy, smoky flavour, which comes from the paprika with which it's spiced. Cooking the chorizo and draining the oil makes it a little healthier, as chorizo can sometimes be a little fatty. I like to keep the skin on the apples, as many of their nutrients are contained in the skin. The tangy, slightly sweet apple balances the spicy chorizo, while the pecan nuts bring the crunch.

1 tsp olive oil
200–300g chorizo, sliced
3–4 granny smith apples, sliced with skin on
3–4 cups loosely packed baby spinach
salt and pepper to taste
1 cup roughly chopped pecan nuts

DRESSING
¼ cup olive oil
2 Tbsp apple cider vinegar
4 tsp wholegrain mustard
4 tsp honey

1. Heat the olive oil in a frying pan and brown the chorizo slices until they just start crisping on the edges. Remove the chorizo from the pan and drain on paper towel.

2. Whisk the dressing ingredients.

3. Toss the chorizo, apples and baby spinach in a bowl and season with salt and pepper.

4. Pour over the dressing and toss until well combined, then scatter over the pecan nuts.

Unique Burger Salad

Most people love a good burger, but trying to follow a healthy lifestyle often means sacrificing such comfort food. That's why I give you the burger salad. I bet you're thinking, 'No way!' But here it is, containing all the best elements of the classic burger: the juicy patty, the sweet and tangy caramelised onions, and even the melted cheese, all held together with crunchy lettuce. Go on, give it a try. Delicious served with zucchini fries.

BURGER PATTIES

500g lean beef mince
1 large egg, whisked
2 Tbsp breadcrumbs
1 tsp Worcestershire sauce
1 Tbsp light chutney
1 Tbsp tomato sauce
2 tsp dried origanum
3 Tbsp brown onion soup powder
salt and pepper to taste

CARAMELISED ONIONS

¼ cup honey
2 tsp lemon juice
2 onions, sliced
¼ tsp salt

TOPPINGS

125g camembert cheese, sliced
1 cos or gem lettuce, inner leaves only
2 tomatoes, sliced
2 jalapeño chillies, sliced
2 small avocados, halved

1. Combine the ingredients for the burger patties in a bowl. Shape into four patties.

2. To make the caramelised onions, add the honey, lemon juice, onions and salt to a saucepan. Cook over medium heat for about 10 minutes until the onions start to caramelise. Remove from the heat and set aside.

3. Heat a non-stick frying pan and fry the burger patties until cooked to preference. You might need to add a touch of oil to prevent the patties from sticking to the pan.

4. When all the patties are cooked, transfer them to a baking sheet and place a slice of camembert on top of each. Switch on the oven's grill and grill the patties for a few minutes until the cheese just starts to melt.

5. Separate the lettuce leaves and use a few per patty. Make a small bed of lettuce, place a patty on top and layer with the caramelised onions, tomato slices and jalapeño chillies. 'Close' each burger with an avocado half.

Creamy Cos and Rump Salad

Ruby-hued smoked paprika, whether from Hungary or Spain, is made from ground peppers. But don't expect the same blow-your-socks-off heat that you get from cayenne pepper or dried chilli flakes. Paprika has a more complex, intense, smoky flavour, which makes it the perfect partner for red meat. The addition of sliced and sautéed baby potatoes is my ode to fries, making this salad reminiscent of the English staple, steak and chips.

500–600g rump steak
olive oil for drizzling
6–8 baby potatoes, finely sliced with skins on
3 cups torn cos lettuce

RUB
2 Tbsp smoked paprika
4 tsp garlic powder
1 tsp ground black pepper
1 tsp salt
2 Tbsp olive oil

DRESSING
¼ cup plain yoghurt
⅓ cup chopped cucumber
2 Tbsp roughly chopped fresh mint
2 Tbsp lemon juice
salt and pepper to taste

1. Mix the rub ingredients. Drizzle the rump steak with olive oil and coat in the rub.

2. Heat a non-stick frying pan until hot and sear the steak on all sides. Turn down the heat and cook the steak to preference – I like mine medium rare. Remove the steak from the pan and allow to rest for a few minutes before slicing.

3. Drizzle some olive oil into the pan you used to cook the steak and sauté the sliced baby potatoes until crisp. Remove and drain on paper towel.

4. Place the cos lettuce on a platter and scatter over the potato crisps. Drape the steak slices on top.

5. Whizz the dressing ingredients using a hand blender and pour over the salad.

No recipe collection would be complete without dedicating some space to delightful, sweet treats. We all need to indulge once in a while, and a delicious dessert is one of the best ways to do just that. In this compilation of fruity dessert recipes, you will find that perfect little something to round off any meal.

Although sometimes a little decadent, these recipes all use fresh and flavourful fruits as their key ingredients. It's important to eat fruit on a regular basis to boost your health, so choose the freshest fruit you can find and make the most of each season's spoils, from citrusy oranges in winter to mouth watering watermelons in summer.

From the more savoury peach and plum caprese salad to the creamy kiwi fruit ice cream, here you'll find something fresh, light, fruity and guaranteed to leave a lasting impression on your family and friends. Whether you're looking for a simple, easy to put together fruit salad for the family or a more lavish ending to an elegant evening, these recipes will round off your meals in style and have everyone coming back for more and more and more.

Fruity
Salads

Very Cherry Berry Salad

This dark and brooding salad is surprisingly light to eat, a dash of alcohol lifting the stakes. It's super easy and can be made beforehand so that you don't have to leave the table while everyone else is having fun. If you don't have Cointreau, another fruit-flavoured liqueur is quite alright. Cointreau is an orange-flavoured triple sec liqueur produced in France. It's made using a blend of sweet and bitter orange peels and has a smooth, crisp taste.

250g fresh blueberries
250g fresh cherries
fresh mint leaves for garnishing

DRESSING
1 Tbsp lemon juice
1 Tbsp honey
1 Tbsp Cointreau
¼ tsp finely chopped fresh mint

1. Mix the blueberries and cherries in a bowl.

2. Combine the dressing ingredients and pour over the fruit.

3. Place the bowl in the fridge for at least an hour to allow the flavours to develop.

4. When ready to serve, garnish with fresh mint leaves.

Minty Mousse

This smooth and airy mousse is as light as a feather. It's the ideal fruity dessert to serve to guests, as you can make it the day before, giving you more time when you need it most. Serve this in attractive glassware so that you can see the beautiful pink hues from the berries. The mint undertones give this a refreshing twist, leaving a lingering cool effect on the tongue. The fresh mint garnish adds a final dash of colour, creating an elegant dessert perfect for any occasion.

½ cup frozen mixed berries
2 Tbsp chopped fresh mint, plus a few extra
    leaves for garnishing
1 Tbsp lemon juice
zest of 1 lemon
⅓ cup white sugar

2 Tbsp water
1 Tbsp gelatine powder
⅓ cup warm water
2 egg whites
1 cup whipping cream
1 cup fresh mixed berries, diced

1. Gently heat the frozen berries, chopped mint, lemon juice, lemon zest, sugar and 2 Tbsp water in a saucepan. Stir until the sugar has dissolved, then remove from the heat and allow to cool before pouring into a mixing bowl.

2. Sprinkle the gelatine powder over the warm water, stir to dissolve and add to the berry mixture.

3. Whisk the egg whites until stiff peaks form and then, little by little, fold into the berry mixture.

4. Whip the cream until stiff and fold into the berry mixture.

5. Pour the mixture into individual serving glasses and leave to set in the fridge, preferably overnight.

6. When ready to serve, gently place the diced fresh berries and extra mint leaves on top.

Zesty Caramel Oranges

Sometimes you have to be a little indulgent and this is the perfect fruit to do just that. The orange zest works remarkably well with the caramel sauce, creating a flavour bomb to pour over the somewhat caramelised orange segments. The addition of flavour-enhancing granulated salt adds another dimension, as the combination of sweet and salty is a real treat for the tastebuds. Before you know it, you'll be asking for seconds.

175g castor sugar
3 Tbsp water
zest of 2 oranges
4 oranges, segmented

⅓ cup store-bought caramel sauce
edible flowers for garnishing
vanilla frozen yoghurt for serving
granulated black salt for sprinkling

1. Heat the castor sugar and water in a saucepan and stir until the sugar has dissolved. Bring to the boil and boil for about 5 minutes.

2. Add half the orange zest, reduce the heat and simmer for about 25 minutes.

3. Dip the orange segments into the syrup, coating well, then remove and set aside.

4. Stir the caramel sauce and remaining orange zest into the syrup.

5. Place the orange segments on serving plates and drizzle over the syrup. Garnish with edible flowers and serve with dollops of vanilla frozen yoghurt sprinkled with some granulated black salt.

Fruity Pancakes

These fruity pancakes are loosely inspired by the classic French dish crêpes Suzette, which elevates the humble pancake into a smart dessert. But no setting flame to food here. Ideally, if you have the time, make your own crêpes so that you can make them as thin as possible, but if you're a little intimidated, store-bought readymade pancakes work just fine. The creamy banana custard is the glue that holds this dish together. The burst of colour is thanks to the ruby-red pomegranate arils and the richly coloured raspberries.

1 tsp lemon juice
1 Tbsp honey, plus extra for drizzling
1 cup sliced banana
4 readymade pancakes

1 cup thick custard
½ cup fresh raspberries
2 Tbsp pomegranate arils

1. Preheat the oven's grill.

2. Whisk the lemon juice and honey and coat the banana slices. Place the slices on a greased baking sheet and grill until they just start to caramelise. Remove and mash roughly.

3. Spread the mashed banana over the pancakes.

4. Add the custard to a piping bag and pipe two parallel lines of custard down the centre of each pancake and fold into quarters.

5. Place the folded pancakes on a platter and scatter over the fresh raspberries and pomegranate arils. Drizzle over a little extra honey and serve immediately.

Piña Colada Salad

Whenever I drink a piña colada, I'm instantly transported to a tropical island with crystal-blue seas, white sandy beaches and coconut palms gently blowing in the breeze. It's thought that this creamy drink originated in Puerto Rico in the 19th century, when the pirate Roberto Cofresí gave his crew this cocktail to boost their morale. This fruity salad has all the elements of the delicious drink, without the kick, so the kids will love it too.

3 bananas, sliced on the diagonal
8 slices fresh pineapple
1 large mango, cubed
2 cups gooseberries or melon balls
1 Tbsp honey
toasted desiccated coconut for garnishing

DRESSING
½ cup crushed pineapple in juice
½ cup coconut cream
¼ cup whipping cream

1. Grease a griddle pan and carefully grill the banana and pineapple slices until char lines appear. Remove from the heat and allow to cool.

2. Once cool, place the banana and pineapple slices in a bowl with the mango and gooseberries or melon balls. Drizzle over the honey, ensuring the fruit is well coated.

3. To make the dressing, using a hand blender, whizz half the crushed pineapple with the coconut cream until smooth. Whip the cream until stiff and fold into the pineapple and coconut mixture, followed by the remaining crushed pineapple.

4. Pour the dressing over the fruit salad or serve it separately on the side for each person to pour their own.

5. Garnish with toasted coconut and serve.

Watermelon Surprise

Watermelon is synonymous with summer, so make this your go-to fruit salad during the hot sunny months. What's not to love about a fruit that not only tastes like a dessert, but also, as its name suggests, has got some serious hydration value, hydrating your body like a sports drink but without all the calories? Watermelon is a whopping 90 per cent water. This pink sensation is beautifully offset against the other equally delectable fruit, giving you a salad that has all the flavours and vibrancy of summer.

400g watermelon, cubed
150g papaya, cubed
150g green melon, cubed
⅓ cup honey

1 cup Greek yoghurt
1 Tbsp lemon juice
crunchy wafers for serving

1. Combine all the fruit in a large bowl.

2. Whisk the honey, yoghurt and lemon juice and drizzle over the fruit.

3. Toss to combine and serve with crunchy wafers.

Kiwi Fruit Ice Cream

Originally known as the Chinese gooseberry, this furry, brown fruit started its transformation around 1904. A New Zealand school principal brought some seeds home from China and gave them to a farmer whose trees started to bear fruit in 1910. It took about 50 years for the fruit to become commercially viable, the result of a name change to something more marketable, the kiwi, after New Zealand's national bird. This remarkably healthy fruit is now available worldwide.

4 kiwi fruit, peeled and sliced, plus extra
  for garnishing
5 egg yolks
¾ cup honey

½ cup cream
½ cup double-cream plain yoghurt
¼ cup roughly chopped pistachio nuts

1. Purée the kiwi fruit using a hand blender.

2. In a separate bowl, whisk the egg yolks with the honey.

3. Gently heat the cream and yoghurt in a saucepan. Remove from the heat and pour over the egg mixture, whisking continuously.

4. Stir in the kiwi fruit purée until thoroughly combined.

5. Pour the mixture into a freezable container and freeze for about 4 hours or preferably overnight.

6. When ready to serve, tip the ice cream onto a platter, place kiwi slices on top and scatter over the pistachio nuts.

Peach and Plum Caprese Salad

If you're French, you traditionally serve cheese after your main meal, followed by dessert. If you're English, you serve dessert first, then cheese. If you're me, you serve them together, in a dessert-style Caprese salad. Yes, a Caprese salad is normally presented at the beginning of the meal, but the balsamic reduction and fruits create a sweetness that makes this perfect for serving at the end. Not to be left out, the creamy mozzarella is an equal partner.

2 large peaches, sliced
2 large plums, sliced
50g mozzarella, sliced
a handful of fresh basil leaves

salt and pepper to taste
balsamic reduction for drizzling

1. Place the peaches, plums and mozzarella slices in a single layer on a platter and tuck a basil leaf in between each.

2. Season with salt and pepper and drizzle with balsamic reduction.

Glorious Granadilla Truffles

These fruity truffles contain all the ingredients of a deliciously decadent dessert: chocolate, cream, nuts and some fruit to ease the conscience. The tanginess of the fruit provides contrast and colour to this rich dessert. These truffles can easily be kept in the freezer and then placed in the fridge before serving, so they certainly won't go to waste. Makes about 30

⅓ cup cream
1 cup granadilla pulp with seeds
860g white chocolate, chopped (keep about 80g aside for coating)
10 small strawberries (or any other berry of your choice), halved depending on size

toasted desiccated coconut for coating
crushed mixed nuts for coating
gold dust for coating
pear slices for serving
lemon zest for serving

1. Warm the cream and granadilla pulp in two separate saucepans.

2. Place the bulk of the chopped chocolate into a bowl and pour over half the heated granadilla pulp and all the warmed cream. Let it sit for about 1 minute and then gently stir until creamy and well combined.

3. Add the remaining granadilla pulp and stir until combined.

4. Refrigerate for a few hours until the mixture starts to set.

5. Once slightly hardened, take about a third of the mixture and, using a small spoon, create 2.5cm-diameter balls with a strawberry in the centre of each.

6. Roll the rest of the mixture into solid 2.5cm-diameter balls. Roll half in toasted coconut and the other half in crushed nuts.

7. Melt the remaining chocolate in a double-boiler and carefully dip the strawberry and nut-coated truffles into the melted chocolate to coat them. Sprinkle over some gold dust and place all three batches in the fridge to harden.

8. Serve with slices of pear and a scattering of lemon zest.

Grilled Peach Splits

This is a twist on the classic American diner dessert. Instead of overripe bananas, I've grilled the peaches to give them a delicious, caramelised texture. Peaches are an ancient fruit, thought to have originated in China over 7 000 years ago. They're high in fibre, vitamins and minerals. They also contain beneficial plant compounds such as antioxidants, which can help protect your body from aging and disease. The riper and fresher the fruit, the more antioxidants it contains.

1 Tbsp olive oil
2 Tbsp honey
1 tsp ground cinnamon
4 ripe peaches, halved
vanilla ice cream for serving

4–5 digestive biscuits, crushed
store-bought caramel sauce for serving
½ cup cream, whipped (optional)
thinly sliced nectarines for serving

1. Combine the olive oil, honey and cinnamon and brush over both sides of the peach halves.

2. Heat a greased griddle pan and grill the peaches cut-side down for 3–4 minutes. Turn and cook for another 3–4 minutes.

3. Serve the grilled peaches with a scoop or two of ice cream, sprinkle over the crushed digestive biscuits and drizzle over some caramel sauce. Add a dollop of whipped cream, if using, and finish it all off with a couple of slices of nectarine. Serve immediately.

DRESSINGS

Honey Mustard Dressing

¼ cup olive oil
2 tsp Dijon mustard
2 tsp honey
2 tsp sherry vinegar
salt and pepper to taste

Combine the ingredients and refrigerate until ready to use.

Blue Cheese and Coconut Dressing

¼ cup crumbled blue cheese
¼ cup mayonnaise
¼ cup coconut milk
1 tsp lemon juice
½ tsp garlic powder
2 Tbsp chopped spring onion
1 tsp paprika
salt and pepper to taste

Using a hand blender, whizz the ingredients until smooth. Refrigerate until ready to serve.

Green Peppercorn Dressing

½ cup green peppercorns
½ cup mayonnaise
½ red onion, chopped
2 Tbsp chopped fresh parsley
2 Tbsp lemon juice
salt and pepper to taste

Using a hand blender, whizz the ingredients, strain through a fine sieve and refrigerate the liquid until ready to use.

Cucumber and Mint Dressing

2 Tbsp double-cream plain yoghurt
¼ cup grated cucumber
1 Tbsp roughly torn fresh mint
¼ tsp lemon juice
salt and pepper to taste

Using a hand blender, whizz the ingredients until creamy and well combined. Refrigerate until needed.

Red Pepper Pesto Dressing

1 Tbsp store-bought red pepper pesto
1½ Tbsp mayonnaise
1 tsp Dijon mustard
2 tsp white wine vinegar
⅛ tsp honey
salt and pepper to taste

Using a hand blender, whizz the ingredients until well combined. Refrigerate until needed.

Ginger Sesame Dressing

⅓ cup olive oil
1 Tbsp sesame oil
¼ cup rice vinegar
2 Tbsp soy sauce
1 Tbsp honey
2 tsp ground ginger
1 clove garlic, crushed

Using a hand blender, whizz the ingredients until well combined. Refrigerate until ready to use.

Spicy Asian Dressing

Lemon Caper Dressing

2 Tbsp capers
1 tsp crushed garlic
1 Tbsp lemon juice
1 Tbsp grated Parmesan
1 Tbsp lemon zest
3 Tbsp water
¼ cup olive oil
salt and pepper to taste

Using a hand blender, whizz the capers, garlic, lemon juice, Parmesan, lemon zest and water. Slowly drizzle in the olive oil and whizz until well combined. Season to taste and give a final whizz. Refrigerate until ready to use.

Peanut Dressing

½ cup smooth peanut butter
2 Tbsp white wine vinegar
1 Tbsp honey
¼ cup coconut cream
2 Tbsp lemon juice
¼ cup water
salt and pepper to taste

Using a hand blender, whizz the ingredients to a creamy consistency. Refrigerate until ready to use.

Spicy Asian Dressing

1 Tbsp fish sauce
1½ Tbsp brown sugar
1 Tbsp red wine vinegar
3 Tbsp olive oil
1 clove garlic, crushed
juice of ½ lemon
a handful of fresh mint
a handful of fresh coriander
1 small red chilli, deseeded and chopped
salt to taste

Whisk the ingredients and refrigerate until needed.

Cucmber and Mint Dressing

Red Pepper Pesto Dressing

Blue Cheese and Coconut Dressing

Honey Mustard Dressing

Lemon Caper Dressing

Peanut Dressing

Ginger Sesame Dressing

Green Peppercorn Dressing

INDEX

Index of recipes and ingredients

A
almonds 27, 66, 98, 101, 133
anchovy 64, 78
Apple, carrot and cabbage 27
apples 10, 14, 27, 32, 149
apricots 27, 101
artichokes 20
Asian duck salad 117
asparagus 66, 118, 127
aubergines 39, 40, 44, 110
Avocado, artichoke and tomato 20
avocados 19, 20, 48, 65, 74, 77, 78, 92,
        98, 102, 110, 113, 122, 133, 124,
        142, 150

B
bacon 64, 134
bananas 161, 162
basil 10, 13, 20, 52, 121, 141, 166
bay leaves 82, 121
Bean salad 13
beans 13, 35, 36, 44, 48, 51, 56
beef 127, 130, 145, 150
Beef tagliata 130
beetroot 18, 114
Beets three ways, baby marrow and
        rocket 18
berries, mixed (fresh and frozen) 157
biltong 137
Biltong salad 137
biscuits, digestive 170
Blue cheese steak salad 146
blueberries 32, 156
bread 31, 43, 44, 60, 78, 150
Breakfast salad 43
brinjals see aubergines
broccolini 35, 128
Burger patties 150
butternut 20, 40, 43

C
cabbage 14, 27, 32, 87, 141
Cajun rub 94
Cajun swordfish salad 94
calamari 74
canola oil 142
capers 47, 59, 70, 137, 173
Caprese salad 10
Caramelised onions 150
carrots 14, 27, 44, 52, 55, 87, 106, 122
cashew nuts 137
cauliflower 23, 47, 59
Cauliflower floret salad 59

Cauliflower, onion and coriander 23
celery 10, 13, 36, 59, 69, 94, 98
Charred greens 35
cheese 10, 13, 20, 23, 24, 30, 31, 32,
        35, 39, 40, 43, 44, 60, 64, 105,
        109, 110, 114, 118, 126, 128, 130,
        134, 137, 138, 142, 146, 150, 166,
        172, 173
Cheesy roast vegetable salad 40
cherries 156
chicken 98, 99, 101, 102, 105, 106, 109,
        110, 113, 114, 118, 121, 122
Chicken frittata salad 105
Chicken nacho salad 113
Chicken satay salad 99
chickpeas 36, 43, 51, 105
chilli 55, 59, 74, 77, 81, 88, 102, 110,
        113, 117, 122, 141, 142, 150, 173
Chimichurri chicken salad 102
chives 14, 59, 109, 121, 145
chocolate 169
chorizo 149
chutney 105, 146, 150
cinnamon 36, 170
coconut milk and cream 94, 99, 121, 162,
        172, 173
coconut, desiccated 121, 162, 169
Cointreau 156
coleslaw mix 99
Colourful chicken and beetroot salad 114
coriander 23, 27, 48, 56, 81, 82, 85, 87,
        88, 98, 99, 102, 113, 121, 122,
        146, 173
corn 19, 44, 122
Corn, spring onion and avocado 19
cornflour 14, 81
couscous 73, 114
cranberry 109, 128
crayfish 77
cream (fresh and sour) 73, 78, 82, 113,
        157, 162, 165, 169, 170
Creamy coleslaw 14
Creamy cos and rump salad 153
croutons 102, 142
Crunchy chorizo salad 149
Crunchy smoked chicken salad 102
cucumber 13, 24, 31, 36, 51, 77, 78, 92,
        94, 99, 105, 117, 121, 153, 172
Cucumber, onion and walnut 24
cumin 23, 36, 47, 77, 82, 98, 101, 110,
        113, 121
Curried chicken with pistachios and
        raisins 106
curry powder and paste 23, 82, 106, 133
custard 161

D
dates 47
dill 24, 36, 39, 66, 69, 73, 74, 109, 138
dressings
    Blue cheese and coconut 172
    Cucumber and mint 172
    for Apple, carrot and cabbage 27
    for Avocado, artichoke and tomato 20
    for Asian duck salad 117
    for Bean salad 13
    for Beef tagliata 130
    for Beets three ways, baby marrow and
        rocket 18
    for Biltong salad 137
    for Blue cheese steak salad 146
    for Cajun swordfish salad 94
    for Cauliflower floret salad 59
    for Charred greens 35
    for Cheesy roast vegetable salad 40
    for Chicken frittata salad 105
    for Chicken nacho salad 113
    for Chicken satay salad 99
    for Chimichurri chicken salad 102
    for Colourful chicken and beetroot
        salad 114
    for Corn, spring onion and avocado 19
    for Creamy coleslaw 14
    for Creamy cos and rump salad 153
    for Crunchy chorizo salad 149
    for Crunchy smoked chicken salad 102
    for Cucumber, onion and walnut 24
    for Curried chicken with pistachios and
        raisins 106
    for Eastern prawn and asparagus
        salad 66
    for Exotic crayfish stack 77
    for Greek salad 13
    for Green pea and lamb salad 138
    for Herbed cranberry and chicken
        salad 109
    for Honey-mustard aubergine salad 39
    for Kyoto salad, The 51
    for Mid-summer blueberry and spinach
        salad 32
    for Moroccan cauliflower salad 47
    for Mushroom, parsley and Parmesan 23
    for Nutty apricot chicken salad 101
    for Olé chicken salad 122
    for Onion salad 14
    for Peachy Parma ham salad 126
    for Peppers, butternut and
        mozzarella 20
    for Pickled and spiced fish salad 82
    for Piña colada salad 162
    for Prawn Caesar salad 64

for Prawn skewer salad 88
for Punchy tuna pasta salad 70
for Quinoa salad 30
for Robot pepper and caper salad 47
for Sesame-coated beef and asparagus
     salad 127
for Sesame-dressed black bean and
     lentil salad 56
for Sesame salmon salad 65
for Shaved asparagus, peppadew and
     chicken salad 118
for Shawarma salad 36
for Shiitake and kingklip salad 85
for Smoked salmon and citrus salad 92
for Smoked trout and tahini salad 87
for Smoky chicken pasta salad 110
for Spiced salami salad 128
for Spicy sirloin salad 142
for Spinach, apricot and almond 27
for Sunday salad with roast beef and
     potato 145
for Tabbouleh 36
for Tahini, cucumber and feta
     fattouche 31
for Thai tofu and noodle salad 52
for Tomato, onion and ricotta 24
for Tuna tartare salad 78
for Venison carpaccio salad 133
for Very cherry berry salad 156
for Vietnamese pork salad 141
for Waldorf salad 10
for Wicked wasabi tuna salad 91
for Wood-smoked bacon salad 134
for Zingy roast carrot salad 55
Ginger sesame 172
Green peppercorn 172
Honey mustard 172
Lemon caper 173
Peanut 173
Red pepper pesto 172
Spicy Asian 173
duck 117

E
Eastern prawn and asparagus salad 66
Edamame, mango and chickpea salad 51
eggs 14, 43, 59, 64, 78, 105, 150,
     157, 165
Exotic crayfish stack 77

F
fennel 77, 82, 92
fennel seeds 70
five-spice powder 117
flour 82

flowers, edible 158
Fruity pancakes 161

G
garlic 13, 24, 36, 40, 44, 47, 51, 52, 56,
     59, 60, 64, 66, 70, 74, 77, 78, 82,
     88, 91, 94, 98, 101, 102, 106, 109,
     110, 113, 114, 117, 118, 122, 128,
     130, 133, 137, 138, 141, 142, 146,
     153, 172, 173
gelatine 157
ginger 36, 56, 91, 113, 117, 141, 172
Glorious granadilla truffles 169
gold dust 169
gooseberries 162
granadilla 169
grapes 10
Greek salad 13
Green pea and lamb salad 138
Grilled peach splits 170
Grilled vegetable stacks 44

H
hake 82
ham 126
harissa paste 43, 55, 60
Herbed cranberry and chicken salad 109
herbs, mixed 27, 73, 118
honey 13, 19, 24, 27, 30, 35, 39, 56, 66,
     77, 85, 91, 92, 101, 102, 106, 110,
     122, 126, 127, 141, 142, 149, 150,
     156, 161, 162, 165, 170, 172, 173
Honey-mustard aubergine salad 39
horseradish, creamed 145
hummus 36

I
ice cream 170

K
kingklip 85
kiwi fruit 165
Kiwi fruit ice cream 165
Kyoto salad, The 51

L
lamb 138
lemon and lime 10, 13, 14, 19, 31, 35,
     36, 39, 47, 48, 51, 52, 55, 56, 64,
     65, 66, 69, 70, 73, 74, 77, 78, 81,
     82, 85, 87, 88, 98, 110, 114, 118,
     121, 122, 128, 134, 137, 138, 141,
     145, 150, 153, 156, 157, 161, 162,
     169, 172, 173
lentils 56, 91

lettuce 10, 31, 60, 73, 81, 82, 87, 102,
     133, 137, 142, 150, 153

M
mango 51, 77, 81, 133, 162
marinades 64, 66, 70, 74, 91, 122, 138, 141
marrows, baby 18, 35, 40, 52, 110, 138
mayonnaise 10, 14, 59, 64, 78, 91, 130,
     134, 145, 172
melon 162
microherbs/microgreens 51, 65, 110, 117
Mid-summer blueberry and spinach salad 32
mint 20, 39, 47, 52, 74, 94, 114, 121,
     138, 153, 156, 157, 172, 173
Minty mousse 157
miso paste, white 127
Moroccan cauliflower salad 47
Mushroom, parsley and Parmesan 23
mushrooms 23, 43, 85, 105, 127,
     130, 133
mustard 13, 14, 23, 30, 32, 39, 59, 66,
     69, 70, 82, 92, 102, 109, 118, 128,
     137, 142, 149, 172

N
nectarines 146, 170
noodles, egg 52
nuts, mixed 169
Nutty apricot chicken salad 101

O
Olé chicken salad 122
olive oil 10, 13, 14, 18, 19, 20, 23,
     24, 27, 30, 31, 32, 35, 36, 39, 40,
     43, 44, 47, 51, 52, 55, 56, 59, 60,
     65, 66, 70, 74, 77, 78, 81, 82, 85,
     88, 91, 94, 98, 99, 101, 102, 105,
     106, 109, 110, 113, 114, 117, 118,
     121, 122, 126, 127, 128, 120, 121,
     122, 126, 127, 128, 130, 133, 137,
     138, 141, 142, 146, 149, 153, 170,
     172, 173
olives 13, 30, 31, 40, 70, 87, 138
onion 13, 14, 19, 23, 24, 30, 31, 36,
     39, 44, 47, 48, 51, 52, 56, 59, 65,
     66, 69, 73, 74, 78, 81, 82, 85, 88,
     91, 98, 102, 106, 109, 110, 114,
     117, 118, 122, 133, 137, 138, 146,
     150, 172
Onion salad 14
orange 14, 27, 40, 47, 48, 55, 59, 92,
     101, 110, 126, 133, 158
origanum 13, 20, 24, 94, 102, 113, 122,
     137, 146, 150
oysters 81

P

pancakes, readymade 161
papaya 48, 98, 162
Papaya, black bean and avo ensemble 48
paprika 23, 36, 43, 59, 94, 101, 110,
113, 121, 137, 142, 146, 153, 172
parsley 23, 36, 47, 55, 65, 69, 73, 77,
82,
101, 102, 106, 109, 117, 128, 137,
138, 172
Parsley, bean and lemon salad 36
pasta 70, 110
Peach and plum Caprese salad 166
peaches 126, 166, 170
Peachy Parma ham salad 126
peanut 14, 99, 173
pears 169
peas 66, 99, 117, 121, 138, 141
pecan nuts 149
peppadew 118
pepper (sweet) 13, 20, 30, 31, 40, 44,
47, 52, 56, 65, 74, 81, 98, 110, 141
Peppers, butternut and mozzarella 20
pesto 10, 65, 172
Pickled and spiced fish salad 82
Piña colada salad 162
pine nuts 114
pineapple 162
pistachio nuts 106, 165
Pizza salad 60
plums 146, 166
pomegranate 39, 47, 128, 161
poppy seeds 35
pork 141
potato 69, 82, 145, 153
Prawn Caesar salad 64
Prawn skewer salad 88
prawns 64, 66, 88
pumpkin 59
pumpkin seeds 59, 60
Punchy tuna pasta salad 70

Q

quinoa 30
Quinoa salad 30

R

radish 92, 117, 146
raisins 14, 59, 106
raspberries 161
Raw pumpkin surprise 59
Robot pepper and caper salad 47
rocket 18, 60, 70, 91, 92, 102, 105, 126,
130, 134, 141, 142
rosemary 40, 105
rubs
    Cajun 94
    for Blue cheese steak salad 146
    for Creamy cos and rump salad 153
    for Smoky chicken pasta salad 110
    for Spicy sirloin salad 142

S

salad leaves, mixed 30, 39, 77, 85, 88,
91, 98, 101, 106, 109, 122, 127,
133, 146
salami 128
salmon 65, 69, 92
Salsa 98
Sassy chicken salsa salad 98
sauces
    caramel 158, 170
    fish 52, 66, 117, 121, 141, 173
    for Saucy scallop salad 73
    for Scandi-style salmon and potato
        salad 69
    for Sweet amd sour oyster salad 81
    hoisin 117
    oyster 66
    soy 56, 66, 77, 81, 91, 99, 117, 127,
        133, 141, 172
    Tabasco 77
    Tomato 150
    Worcestershire 150
Saucy scallop salad 73
scallops 73
Scandi-style salmon and potato salad 69
sesame oil 52, 56, 91, 117, 141, 172
Sesame salmon salad 65
sesame seeds 51, 65, 87, 117, 118,
127, 133
Sesame-coated beef and asparagus
    salad 127
Sesame-dressed black bean and lentil
    salad 56
Shaved asparagus, peppadew and chicken
    salad 118
Shawarma salad 36
Shiitake and kingklip salad 85
sirloin 142
Smoked salmon and citrus salad 92
Smoked trout and tahini salad 87
Smoky chicken pasta salad 110
Spiced salami salad 128
Spicy calamari salad 74
Spicy sirloin salad 142
spinach 27, 32, 36, 40, 43, 44, 52, 60,
70, 94, 113, 114, 118, 121, 141,
145, 149
Spinach, apricot and almond 27
sprouts, bean 52, 60, 117, 141
sriracha 52, 56
steak 146, 153
strawberries 169
sugar 14, 20, 24, 52, 81, 82, 110, 133,
157, 158, 173
Sunday salad with roast beef and
    potato 145
sunflower seeds 133
Sweet and sour oyster salad 81
swordfish 94

T

Tabbouleh 36
tahini 31, 47, 87
Tahini, cucumber and feta fattouche 31
tequila 122
Thai coconut chicken salad 121
Thai tofu and noodle salad 52
thyme 40, 85, 91, 94, 105, 109,
130, 138
tofu 52
tomato 10, 13, 20, 24, 30, 36, 44, 48,
56, 60, 70, 74, 82, 88, 91, 102,
105, 113, 114, 122, 130, 142, 150
tomato paste 128
Tomato, onion and ricotta 24
toppings for Unique burger salad 150
tortilla chips 113
trout 87
truffle oil 130
tuna 70, 78, 91
Tuna tartare salad 78
turmeric 36, 82

U

Unique burger salad 150

V

venison 133
Venison carpaccio salad 133
Very cherry berry salad 156
Vietnamese pork salad 141
vinegar 13, 14, 18, 20, 23, 24, 30, 32,
35, 40, 44, 47, 51, 56, 59, 77, 78,
81, 82, 88, 92, 94, 101, 102, 105,
106, 109, 126, 127, 128, 130, 133,
137, 141, 142, 146, 149, 166,
172, 173

W

wafers, crunchy 162
Waldorf salad 10
walnuts 10, 24, 32, 126, 134
wasabi paste 91
watercress 43, 60, 117, 126
watermelon 162
Watermelon surprise 162
Wicked wasabi tuna salad 91
wine 70, 73, 74, 88
Wood-smoked bacon salad 134

Y

yoghurt 69, 91, 102, 106, 118, 130,
134, 153, 158, 162, 165, 172

Z

za'atar spice 85
Zesty caramel oranges 158
Zingy roast carrot salad 55